No firefighters were not harmed in the making of this book.

To work in fire is to indulge in pyromania. There are no ifs, ands, or buts about it. The sparkle of a flame that ascends elegantly off organic material is innately mesmerizing. There is a psychoactive component to watching it, which explains why humans have developed such a deep relationship with this earthly element over thousands of years. One such case was the relationship between fire and the Native peoples on North American soil, pre-mid-1800s. This relationship may have involved fire for war, yes, but also for returning nitrogen to the soil. It was a relationship not rid of consequences, but full of bountiful consequence that would enrich the lives of many species, not only our own. Today, we formalize our relationship with fire. We fight. We prevent. We federally emergency manage through associations with branches, divisions, and sectors. But that innate impulse of wonder for the wandering flame still remains. We long for a deeper relationship with the element that can, too, destroy, but also provide.

My relationship with fire occurs seasonally. It starts in the spring and ends in the fall. It means watching the weather open up and the land become lush and green. It means running in a pack, training and suffering together with people, many of whom you've only just met. It means getting to know a small group of people inside a truck. It entails making endless piles of thin trees under the beating sun, spitting out wood chips for hours. Sometimes it means digging a line in the dirt, tucking your chin tight to your chest to avoid the heat licking your exposed ears. Other times, it means sliding your hands through ash or scooping boiling dirt to locate burning material, much like a detective. It means making precise cuts in towering, marvelous trees, toppling them to the Earth.

It means clocking in during your dreams, cutting fire line until you wake, only to do it again. It means sleeping for meager hours in open lawns and dirt pits, gasping awake in the wee hours, thinking you've overslept. It means being constantly thanked by people you've never met, yet feeling as though you've done nothing at all. It means loneliness despite being surrounded by a family. It means bearing witness to human and landscape deprivation. It means loving your job but hating how stressful and dangerous it can be. It means hating your job but loving that you are in corners of the country that no one else steps foot in, outside, working with your hands. Many days, it means questioning your life's decisions.

Yet, when the late season rolls around and you're standing around a pile burn in October, telling jokes and eating chili, it feels as though many of your choices have aligned in the right direction. My relationship with fire means burning as best you can, even if it's raining. It even means slogging through snow to lay flame under piles of those thin trees you'd been cutting all summer. Then, the next year, you return to the plot of land you know so intimately for sprouting Morels, hoping to see even one Matsutake. Therein lies new growth in a decimated land.

That sparkle in the wisp of flame, the same one seen millions of years ago by many, is the reason we walk toward the fire when others walk away. History has told us of its pains. Many have shared tales of loss. This work remains undervalued, like many other branches of forest and public land management, yet we march on. Through the flame and flurry, we carry them both in our hearts and minds. We will do our best when no one else will. This is my relationship with fire.

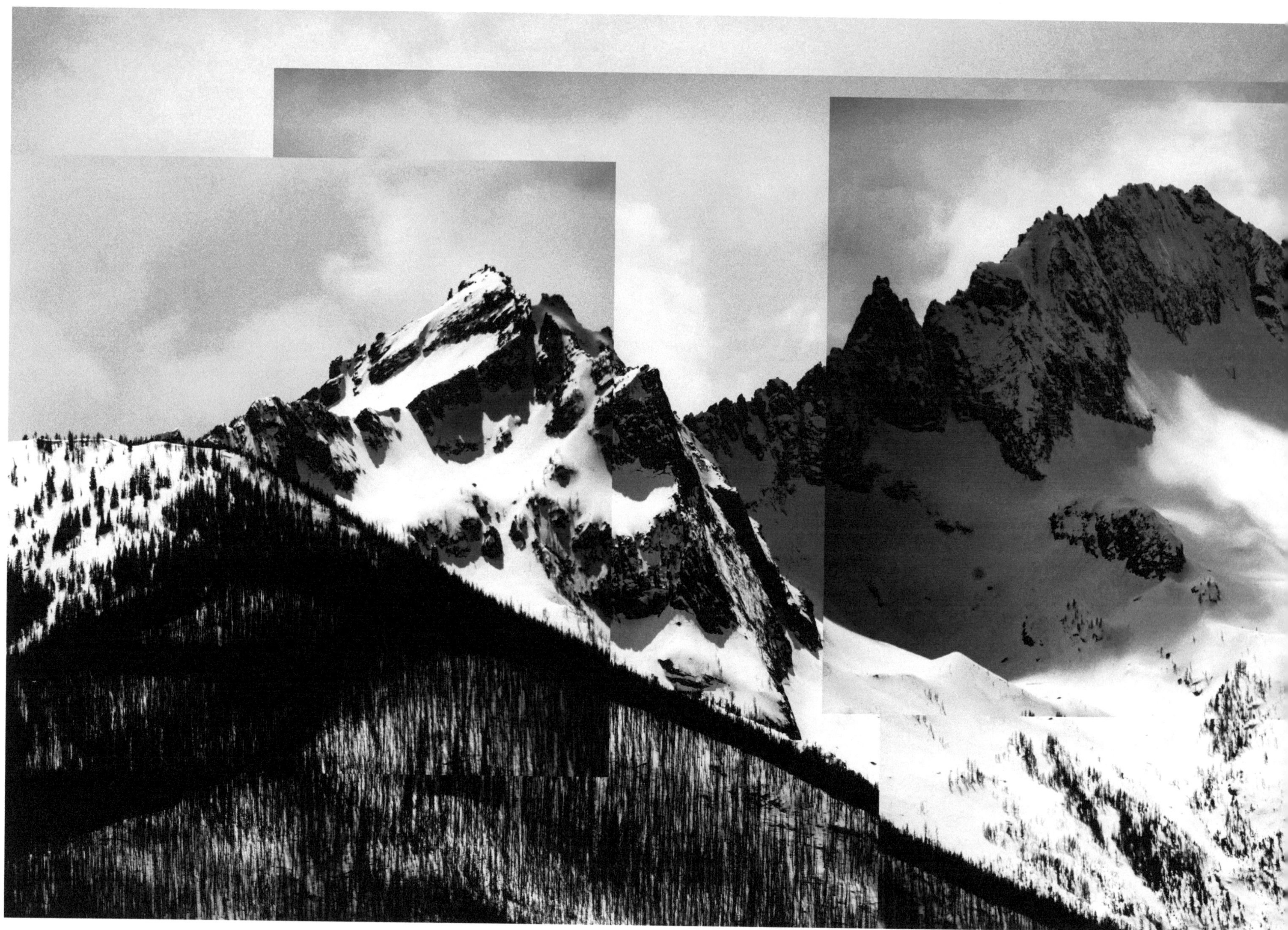

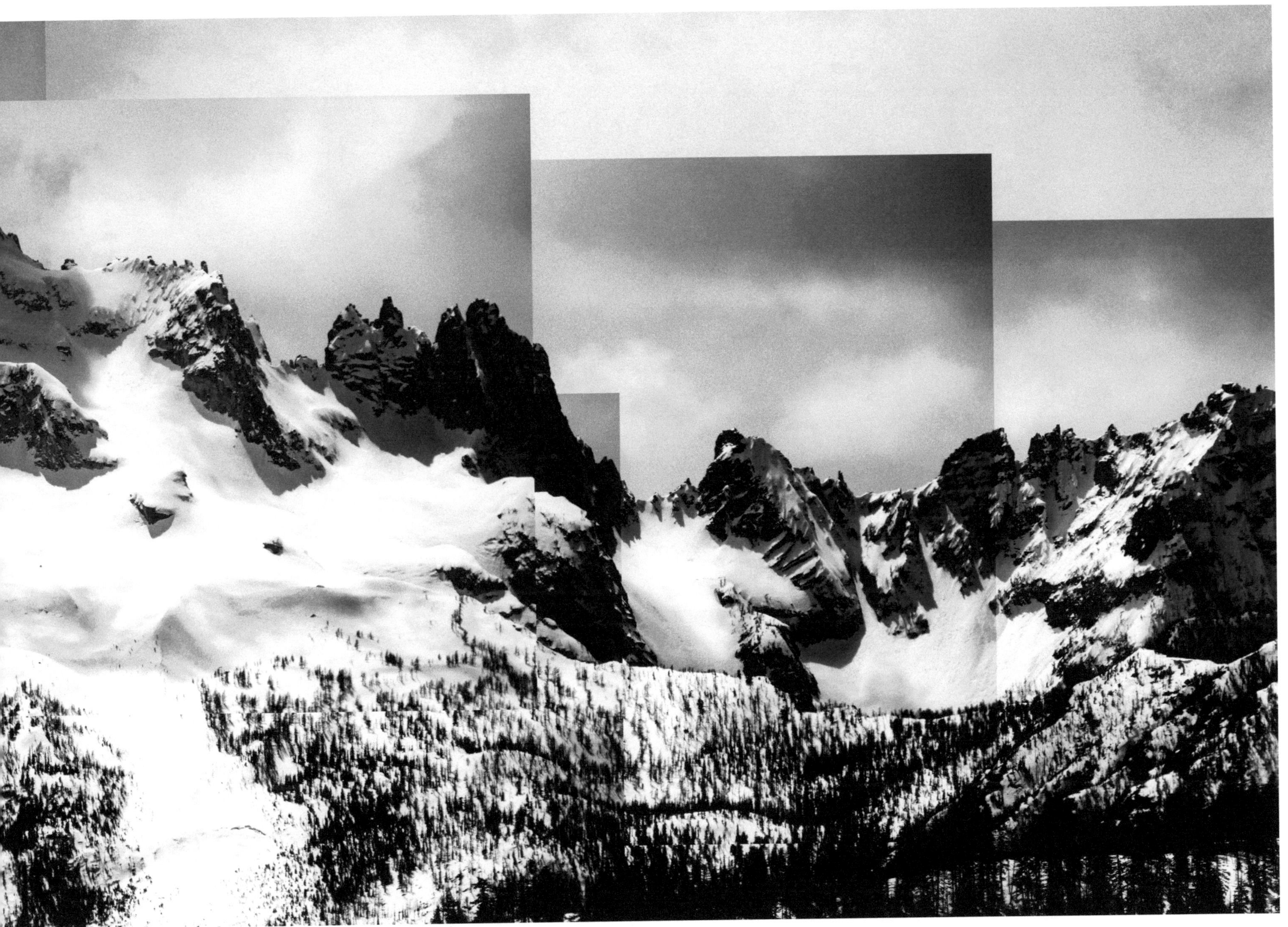

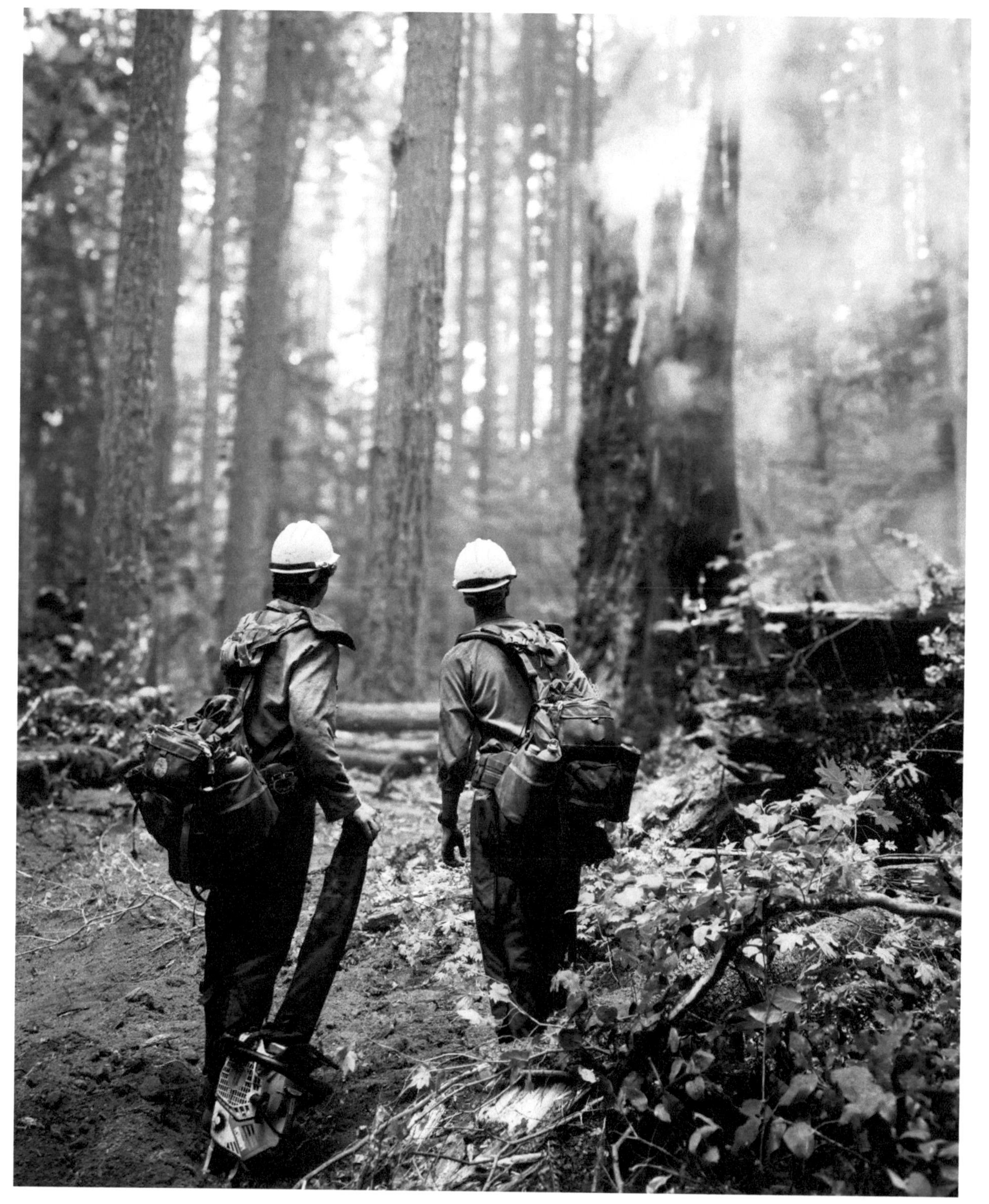

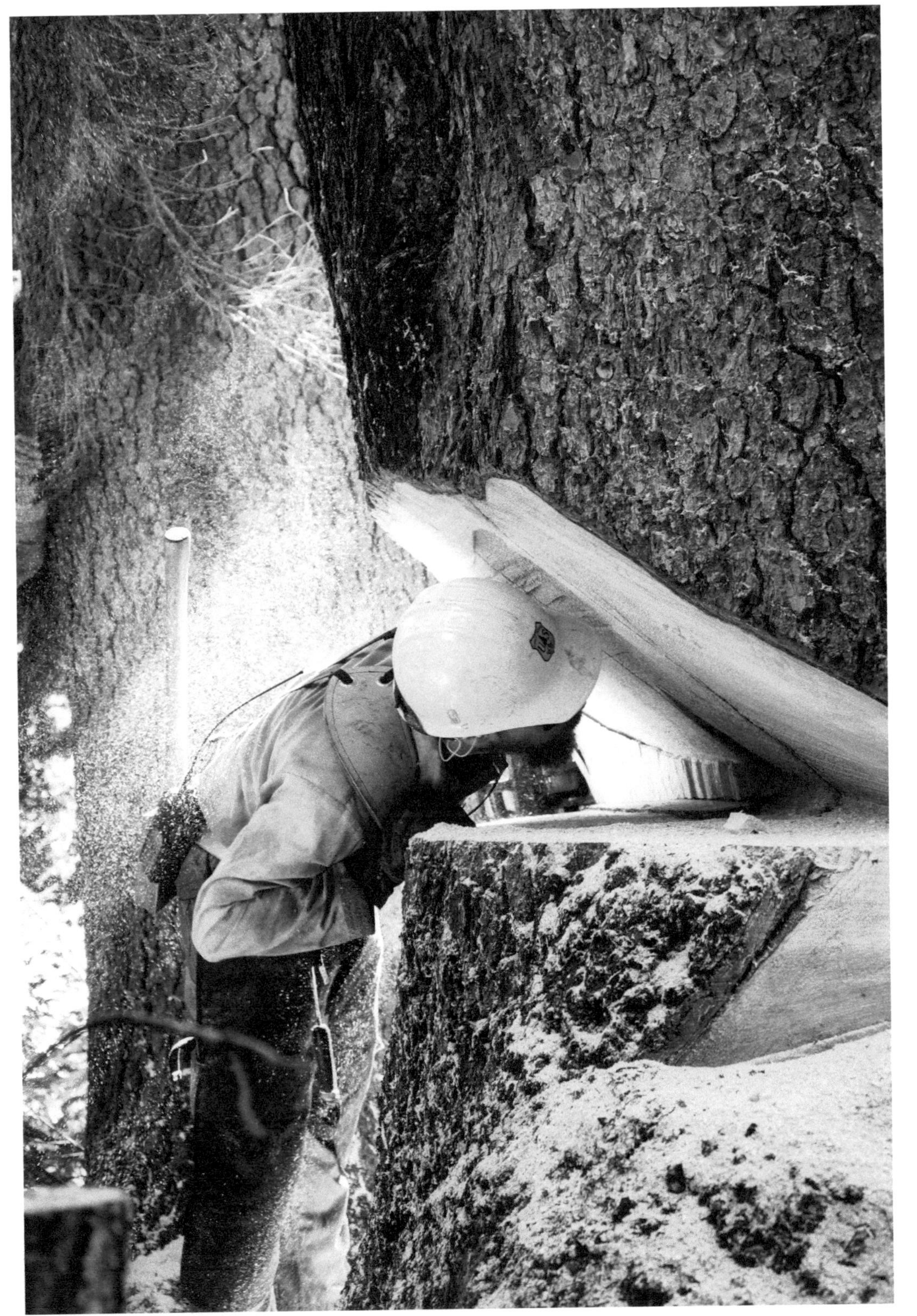

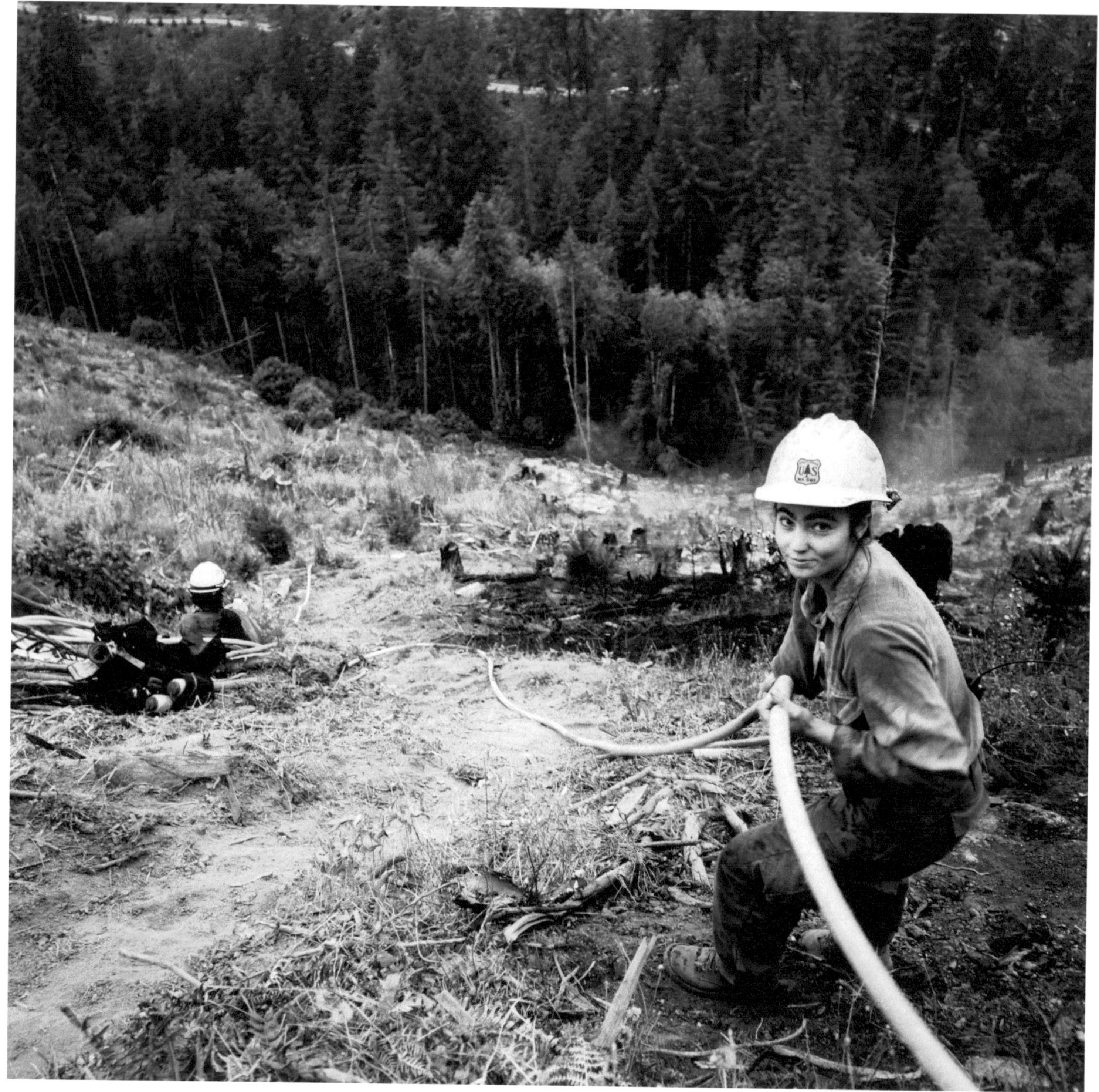

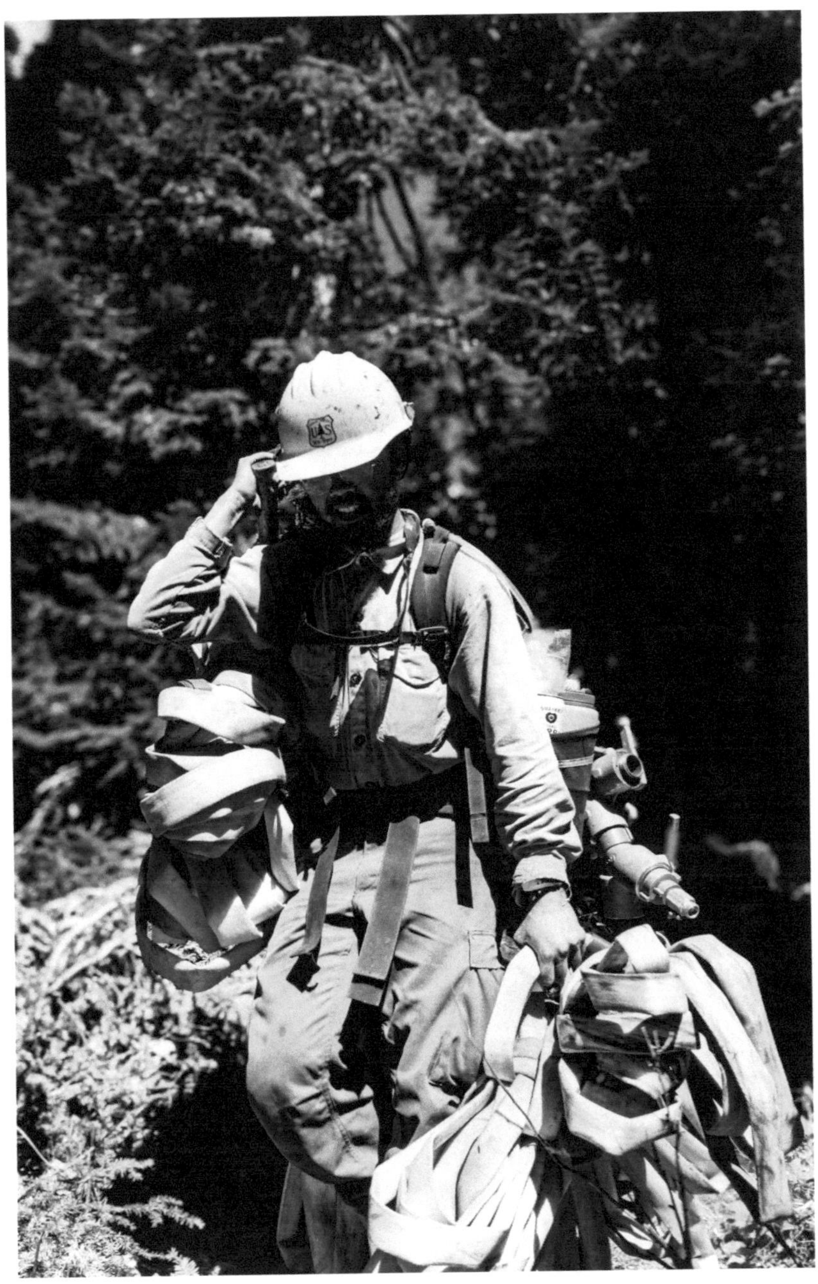
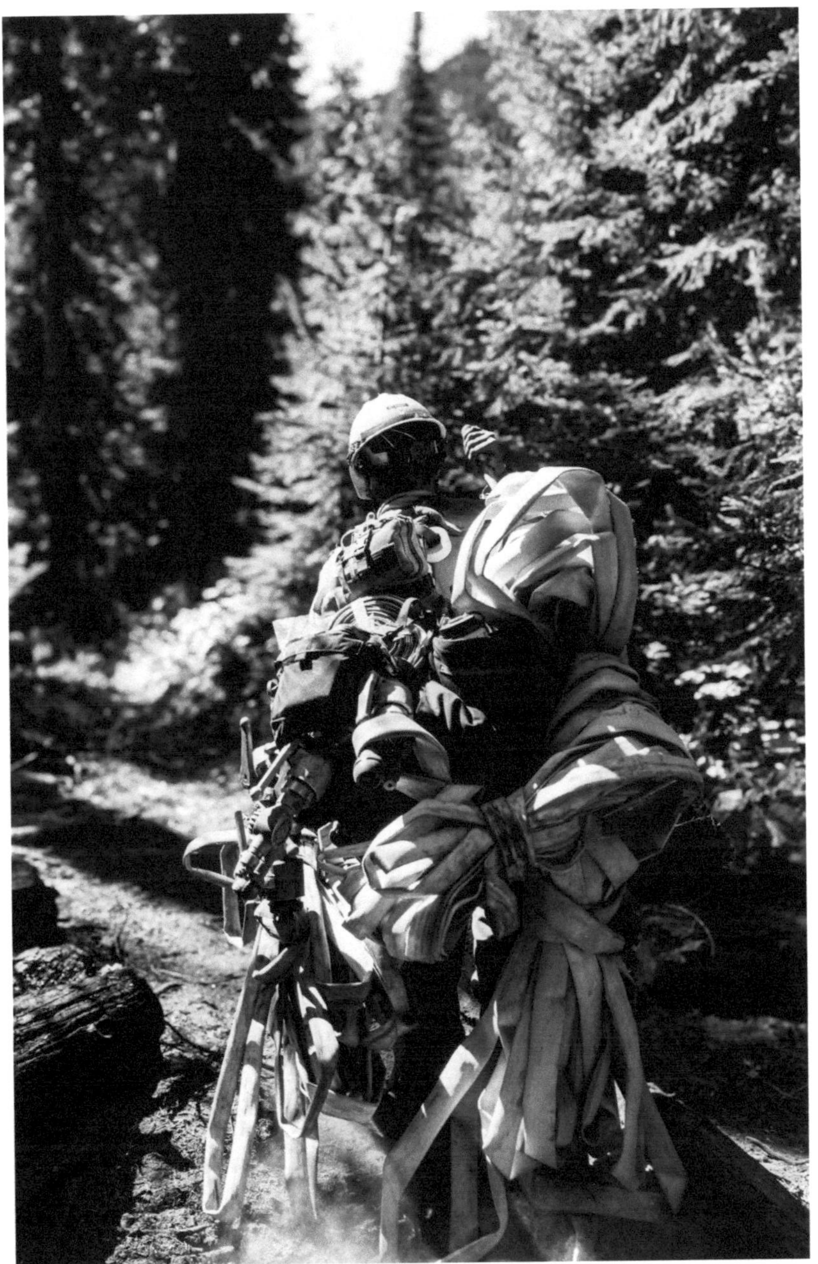

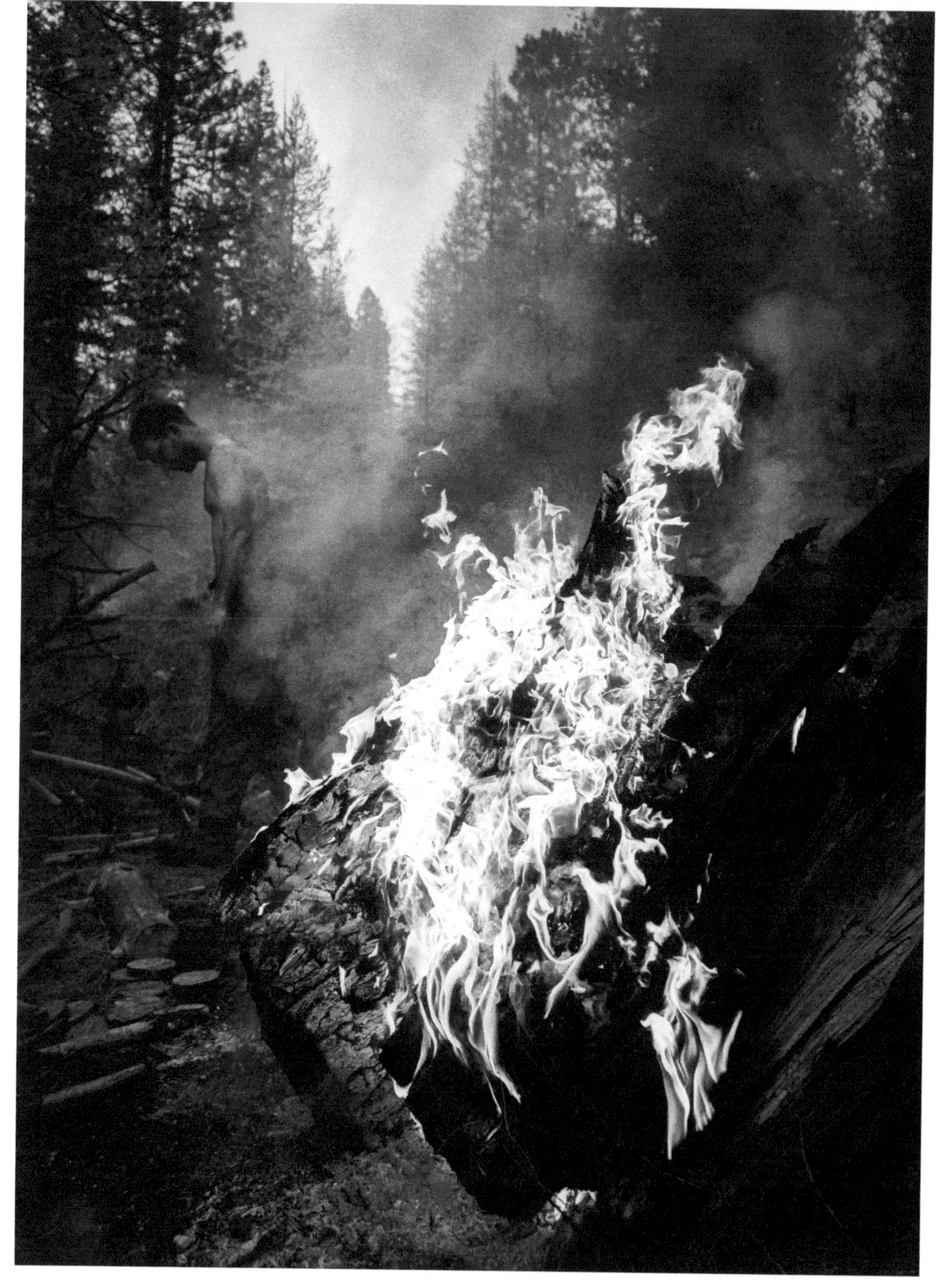

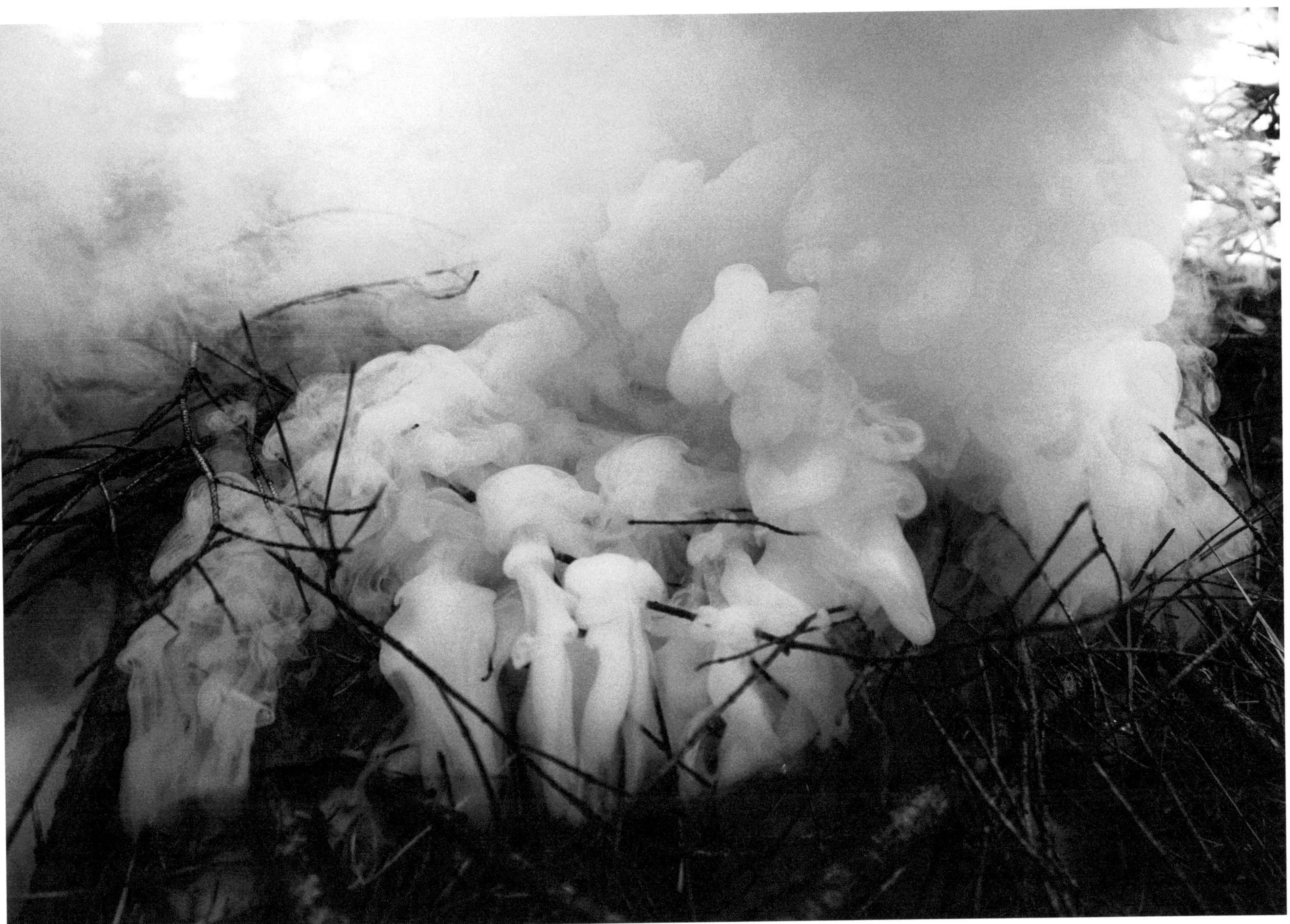

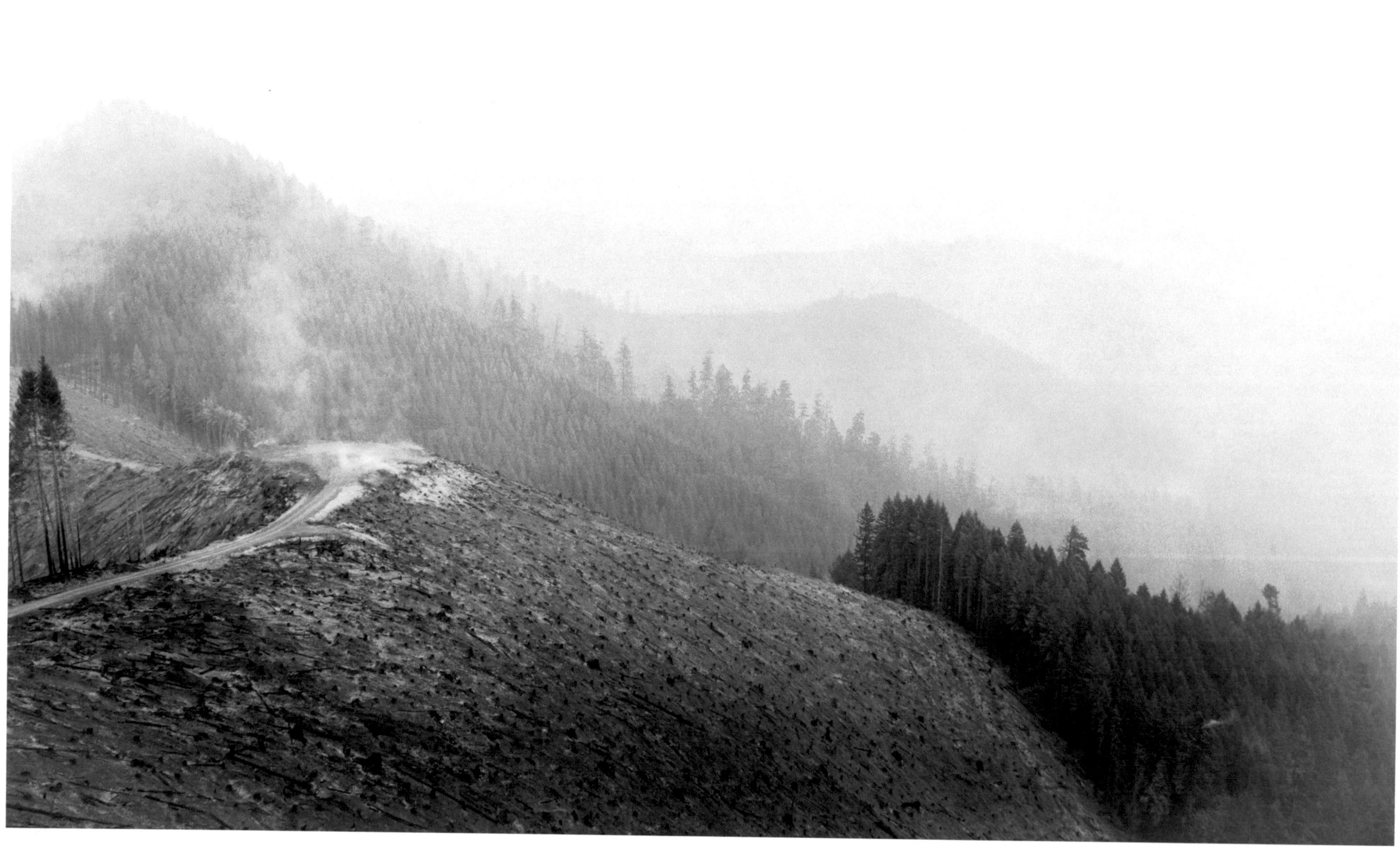

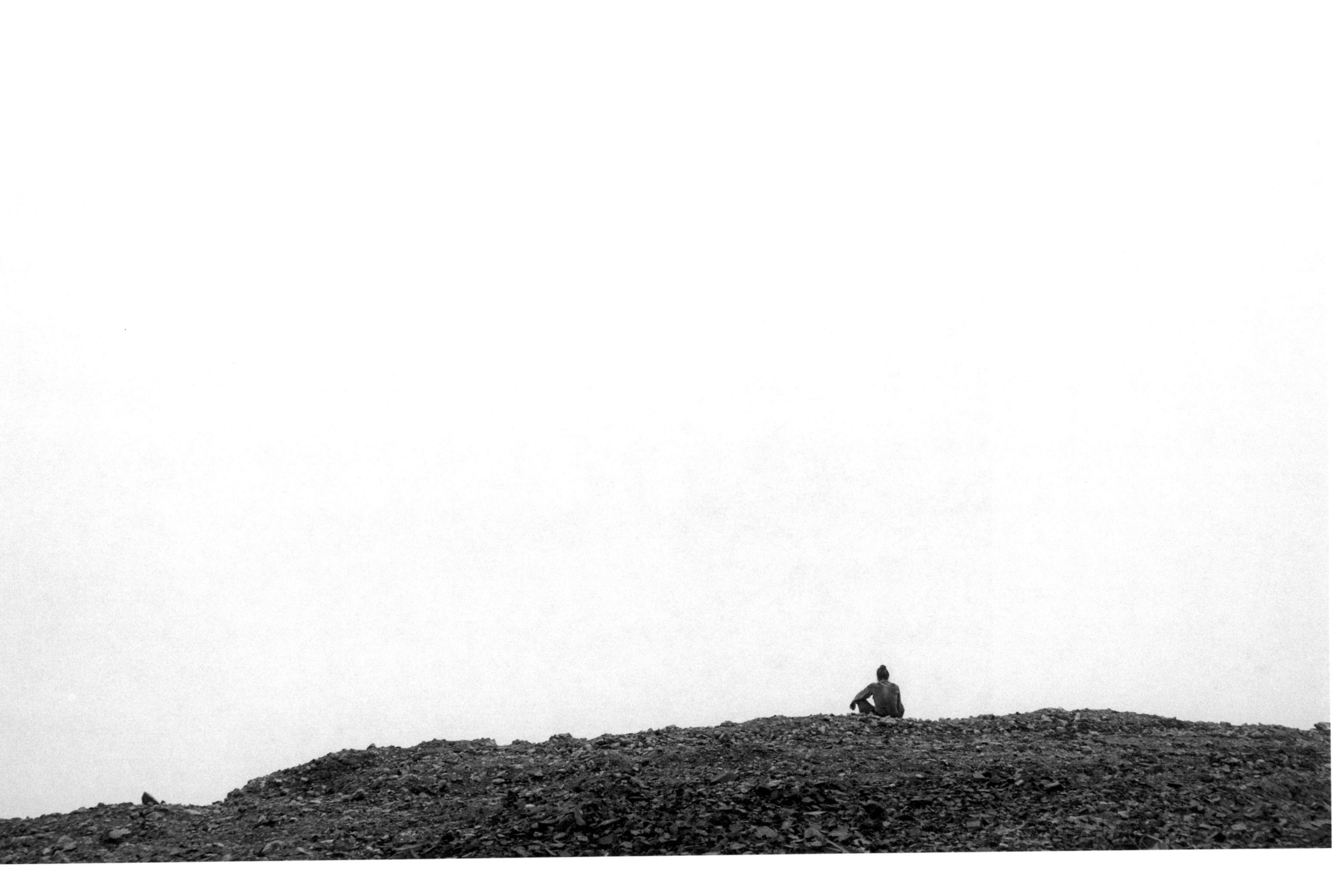

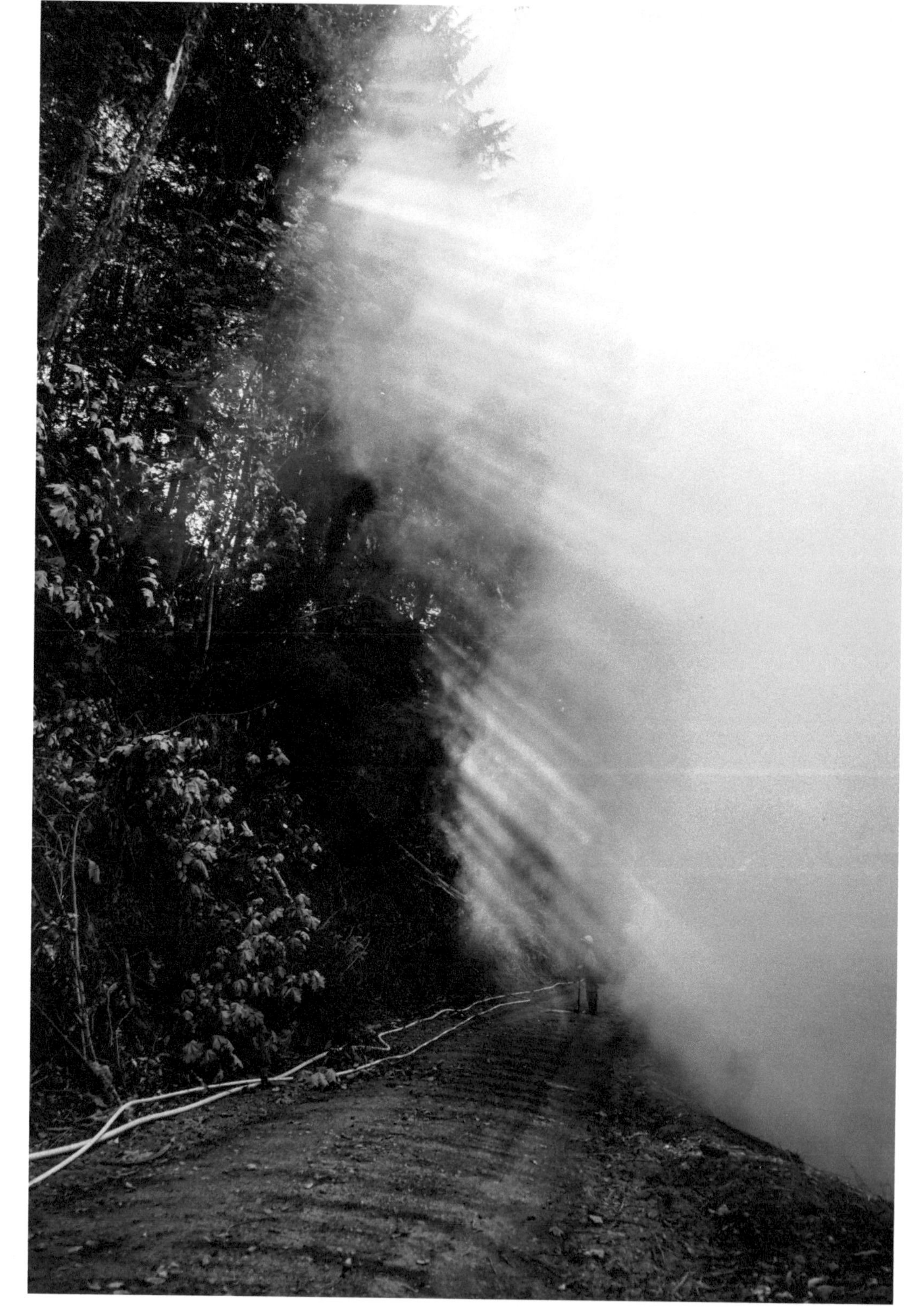

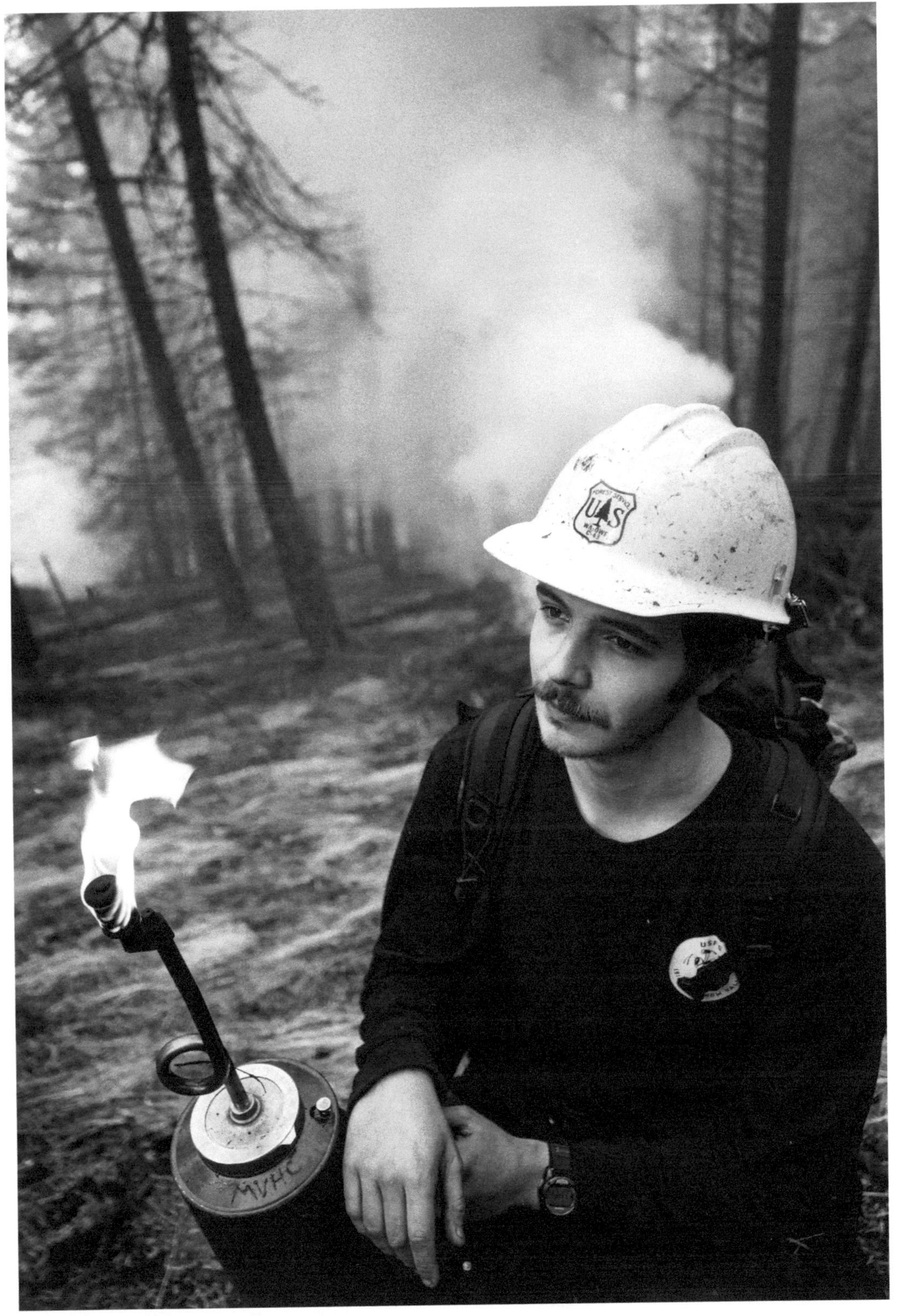

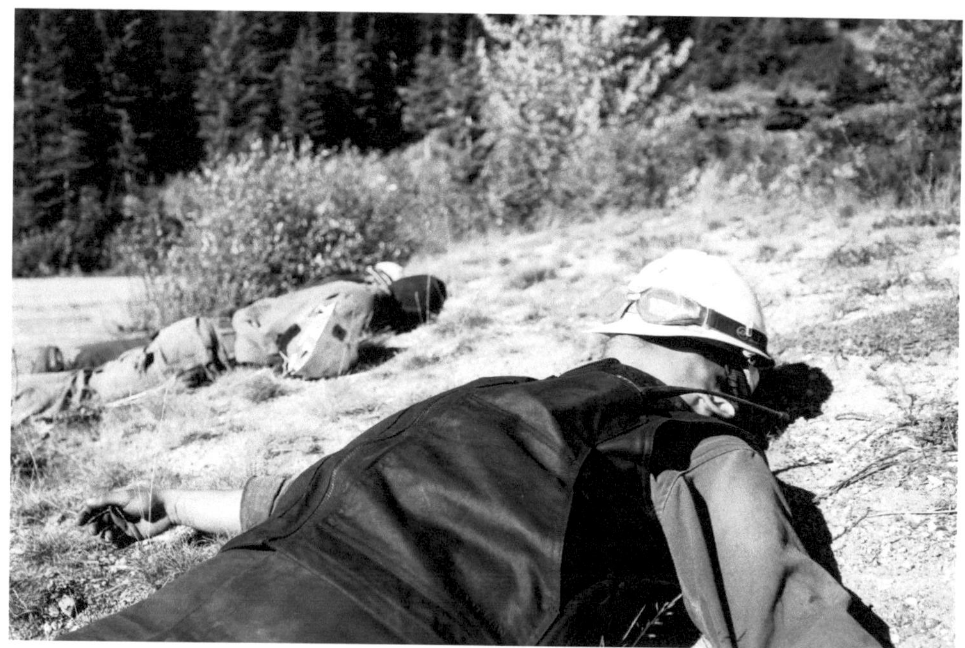

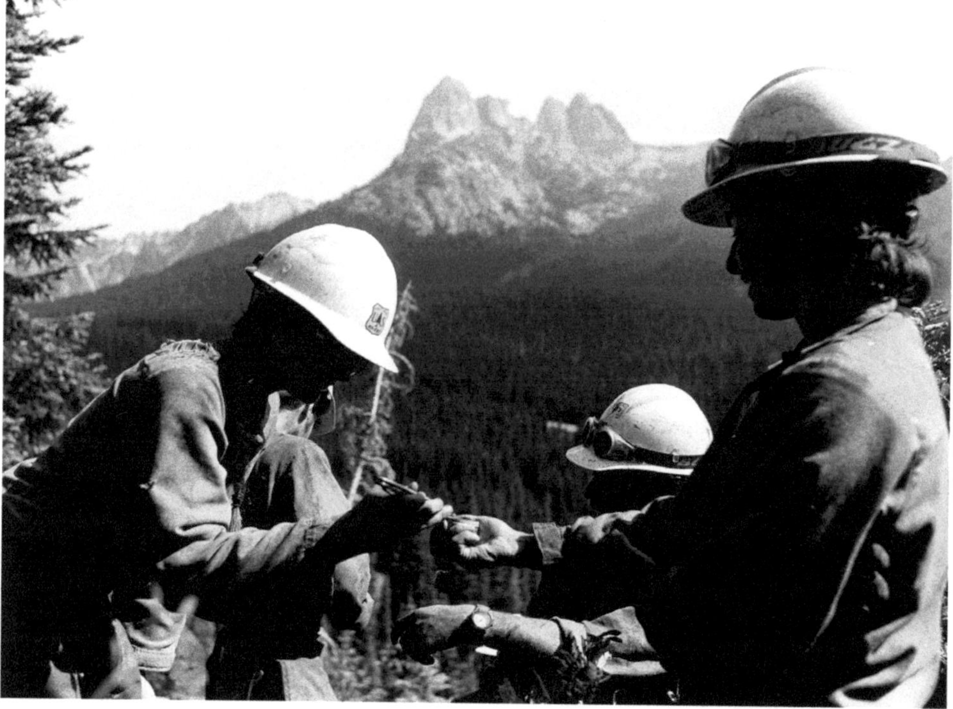

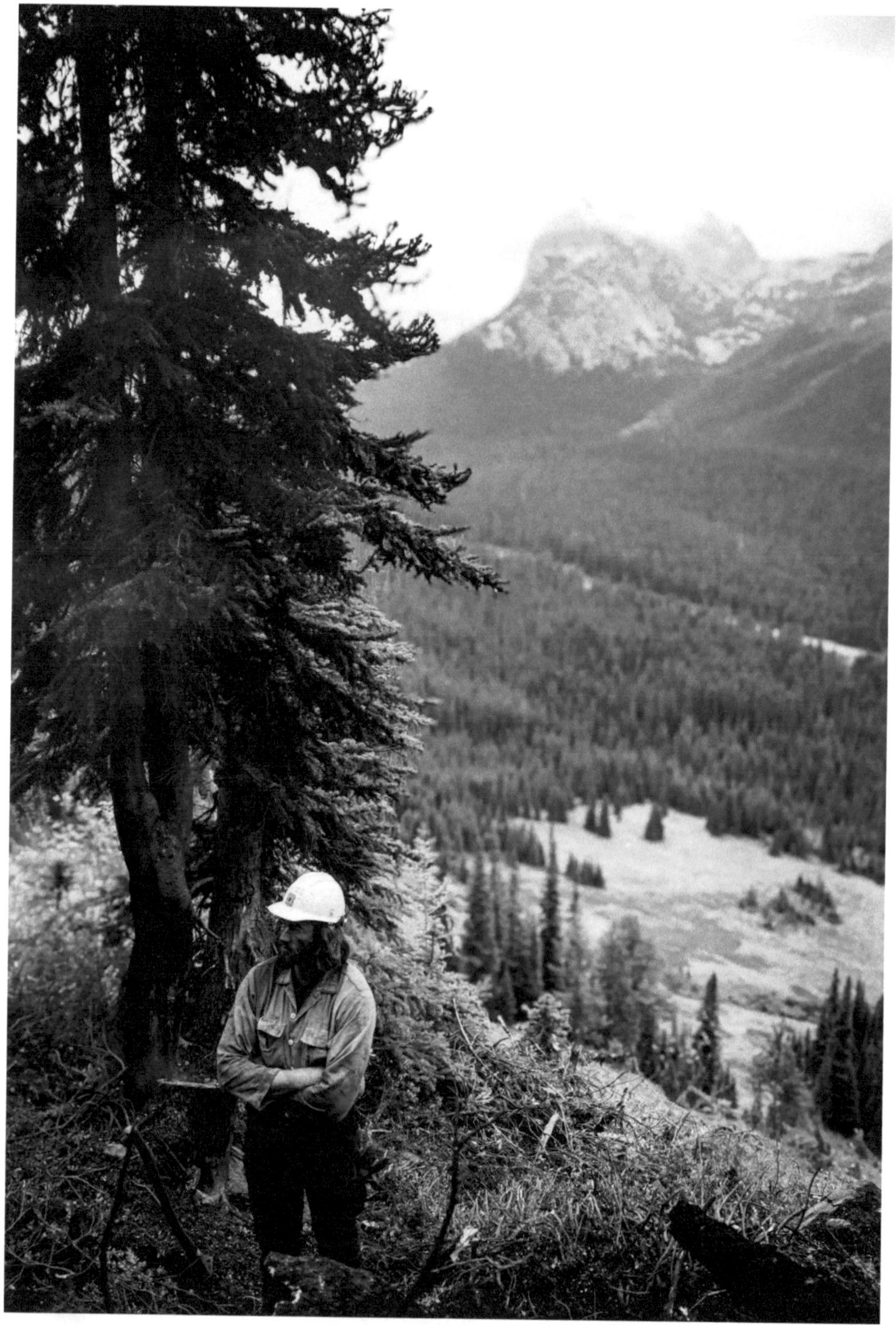

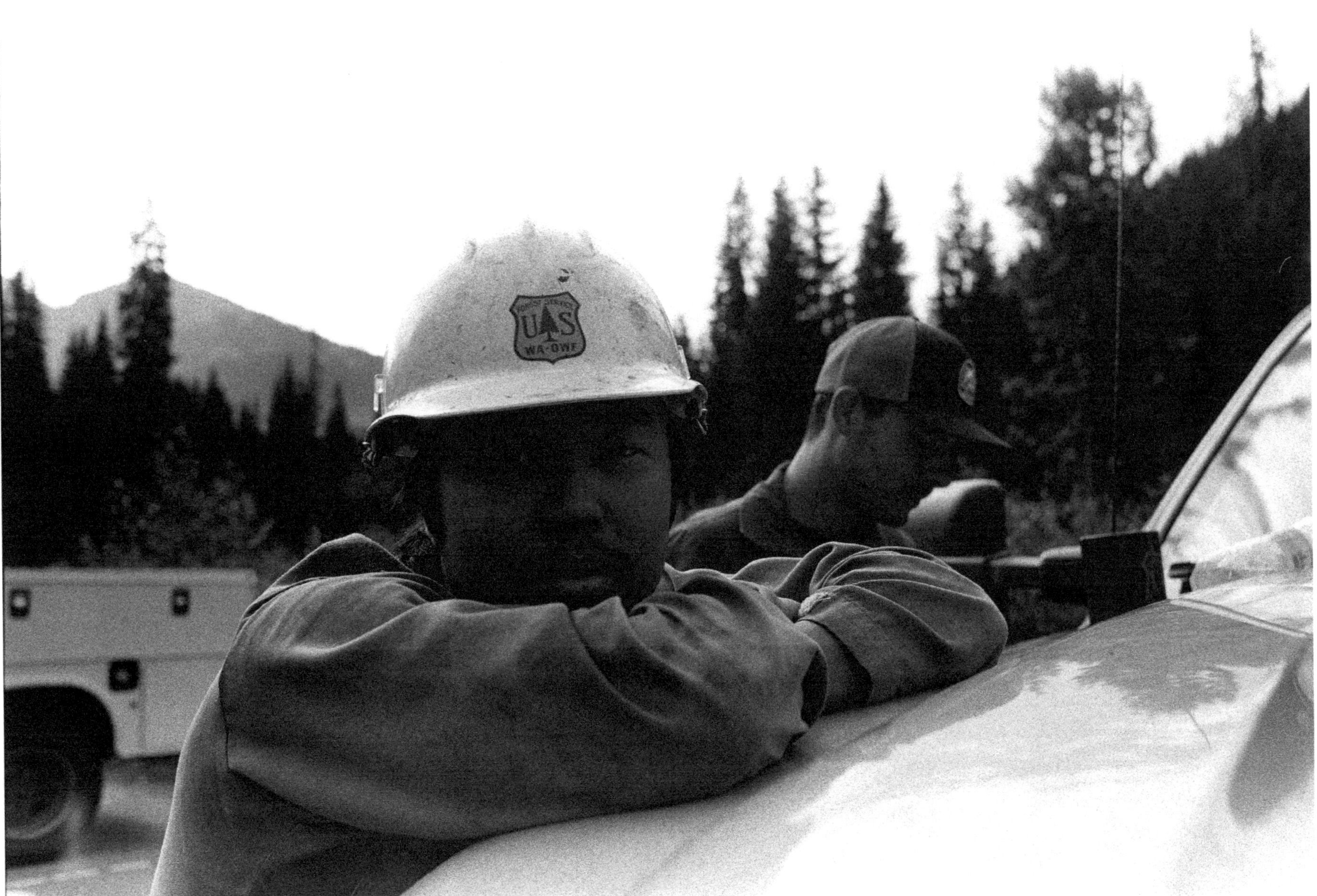

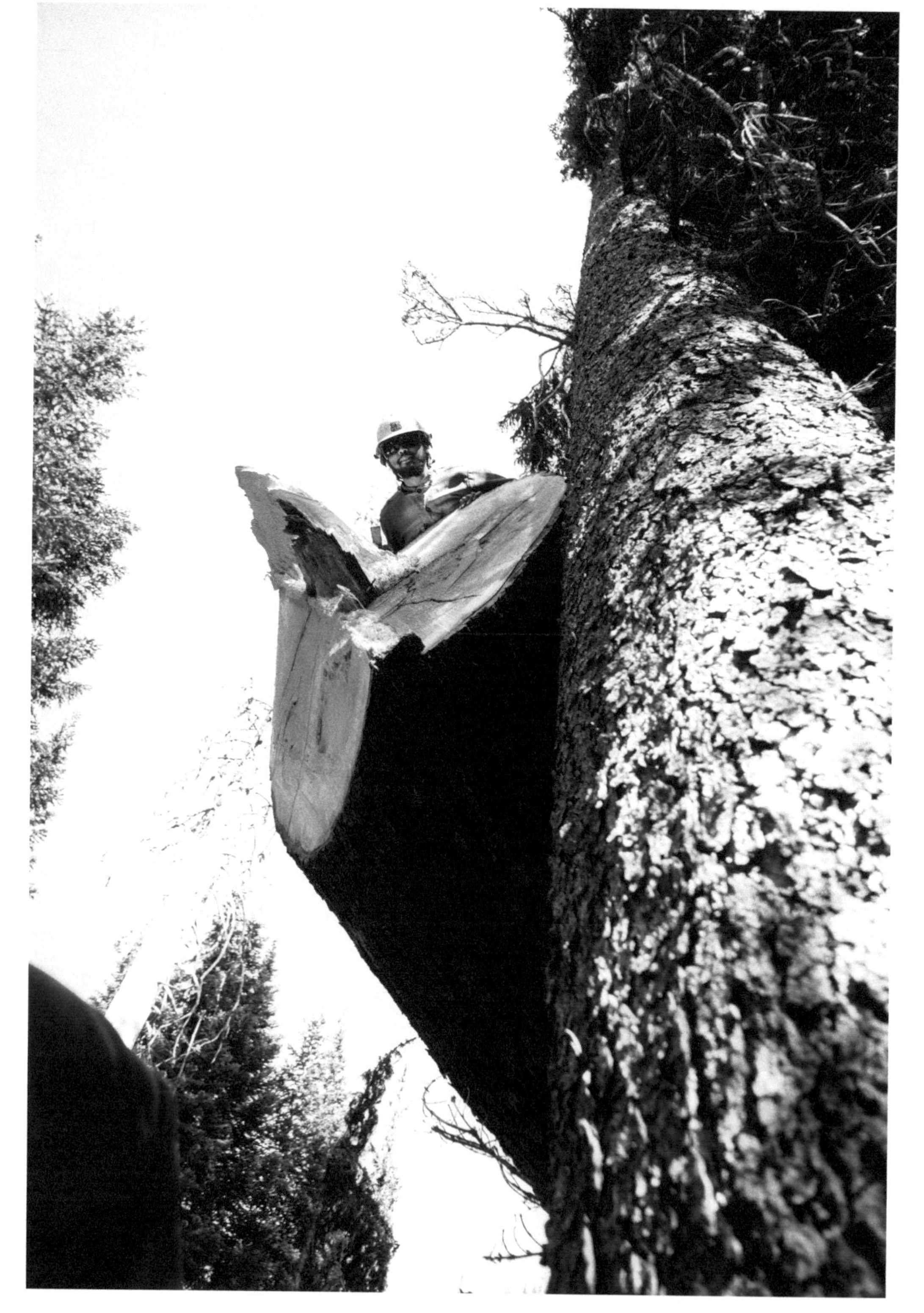

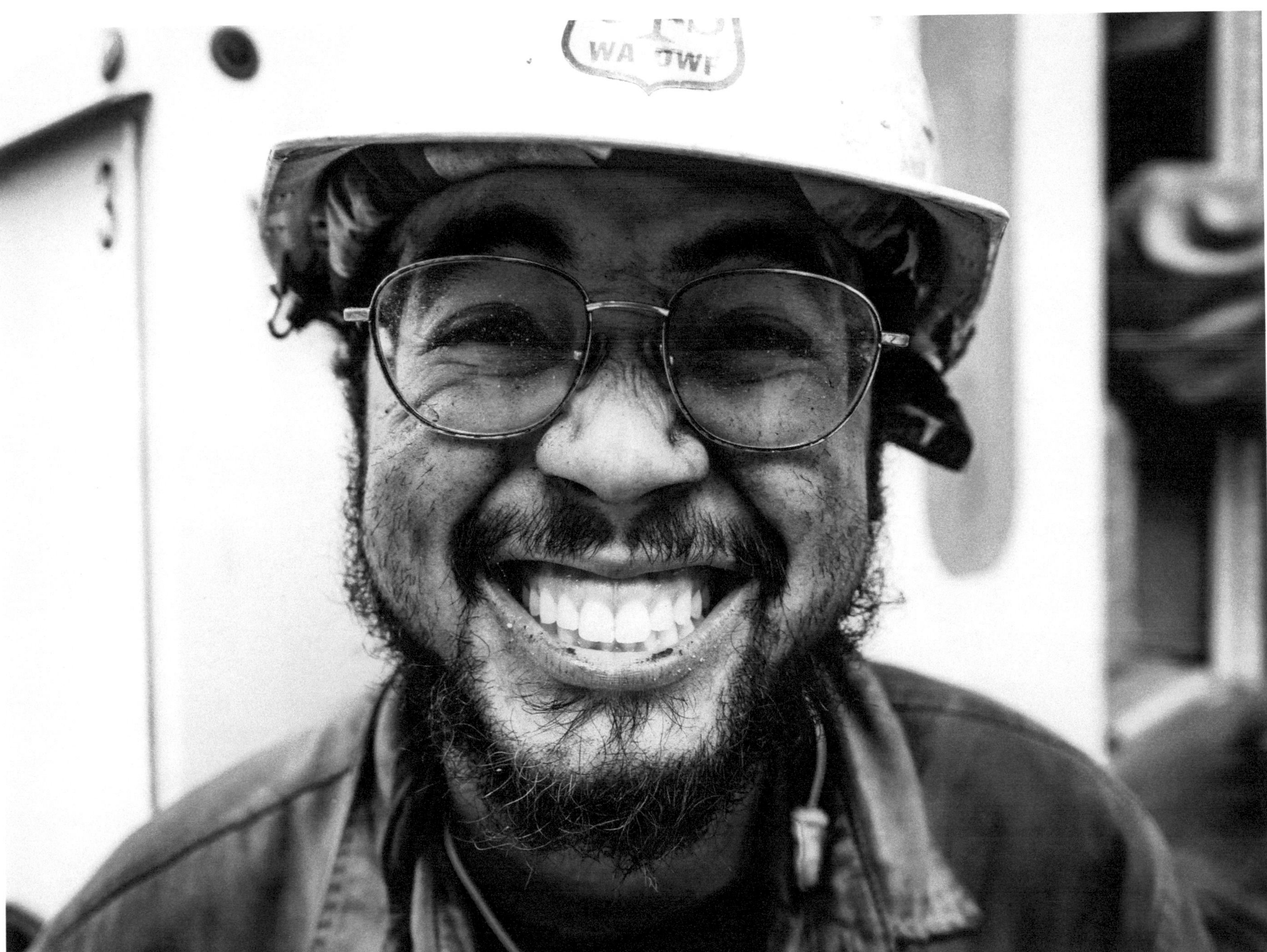

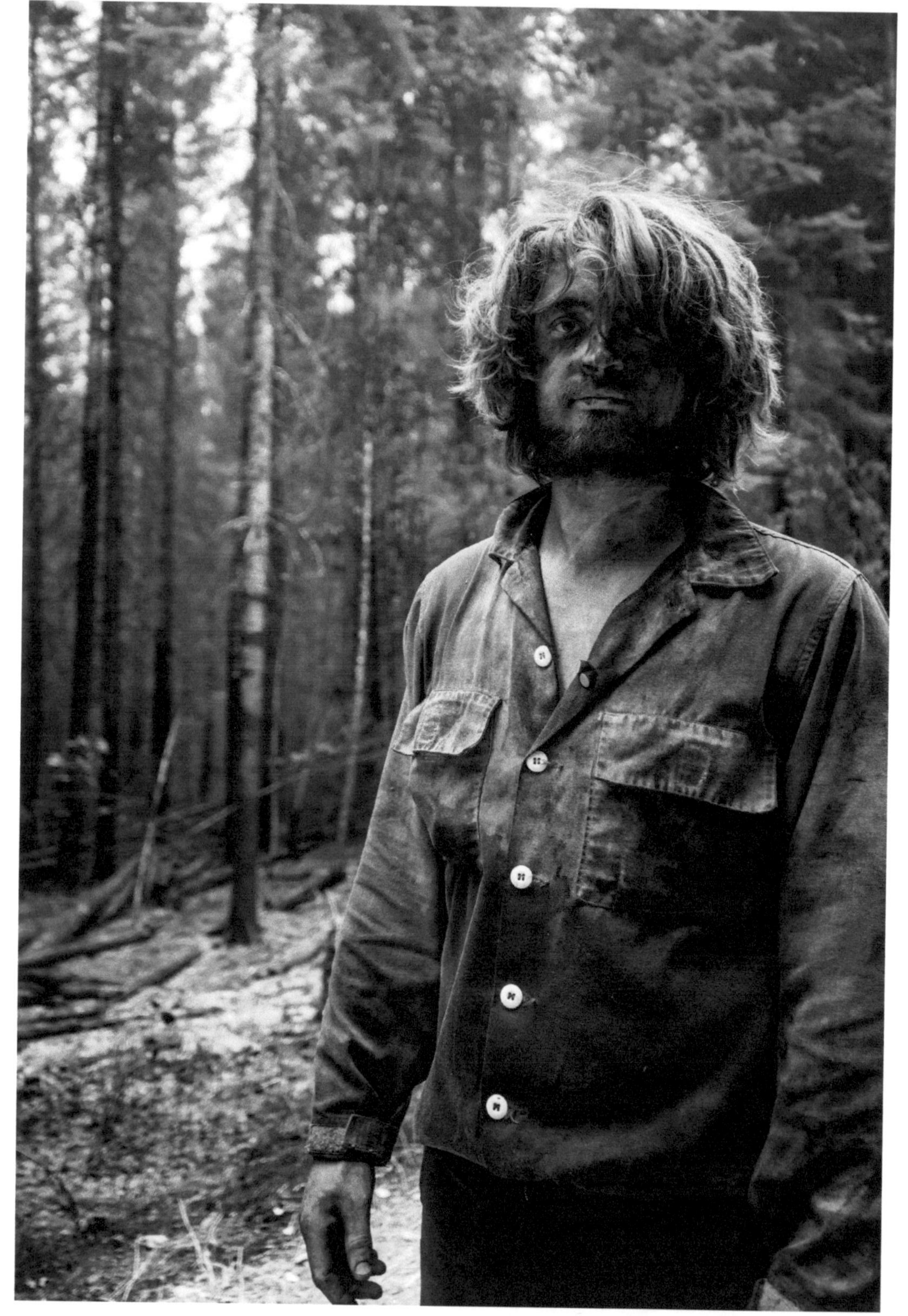

II.

The filth of a wildland firefighter's shirt is an emblem of pride—a badge that says, "I work harder than the rest." The firefighter with the dirtiest yellow is, of course, the hardest working, or they are the best at rubbing dirt on their body when no one is looking. In the wildland community, the filthiness of a yellow commands unspoken respect. If your yellow is spotless, then you probably didn't get your hands dirty either. And if you weren't getting your hands dirty, what were you doing all day? Playing with your schmeckle instead of helping the cause? In this logic, damaged yellows represent those who have hiked the chainsaw, chewed wood chips, and spat dirt. They've seen the edge and back. Yet, no matter how foul the yellow, the buttons remain clean.

Tristan humbly accepts my request for a photo. With his back to the sun, I hope to capture a glimmer of his aura that afternoon. He does not smile, nor do I ask that of him. Tristan had just escaped a falling western hemlock tree, which reminds me of the reality involved in working in a burning forest. Western hemlock trees smolder at the roots and in the surrounding duff. With no taproot to keep it upright, this is the tree that falls silent like a hushed crowd. The roots were so compromised that we'd been pushing trees over by hand that day. After Tristan's near miss, we joked that he wasn't allowed to drive after it thwacked his hardhat off because we didn't know if he had a concussion or not. But in earnest, this was no joke.

Risk of injury is something we inherently take on as we head to the fireline. Many may take on the job because there is risk involved. Damaged, deranged, pyromaniac—we accept all these diagnoses. We accept that it's a job that must be done, and while statistics of injury and fatality are outweighed by success and lifelong careers, the number is not zero. I would ask anyone wanting to commit to even one season in this job if they thought the romantic idea of risk was truly worth chasing. Did you just want the summer paycheck? The dirtiest yellow? Or is there something that can keep you longer?

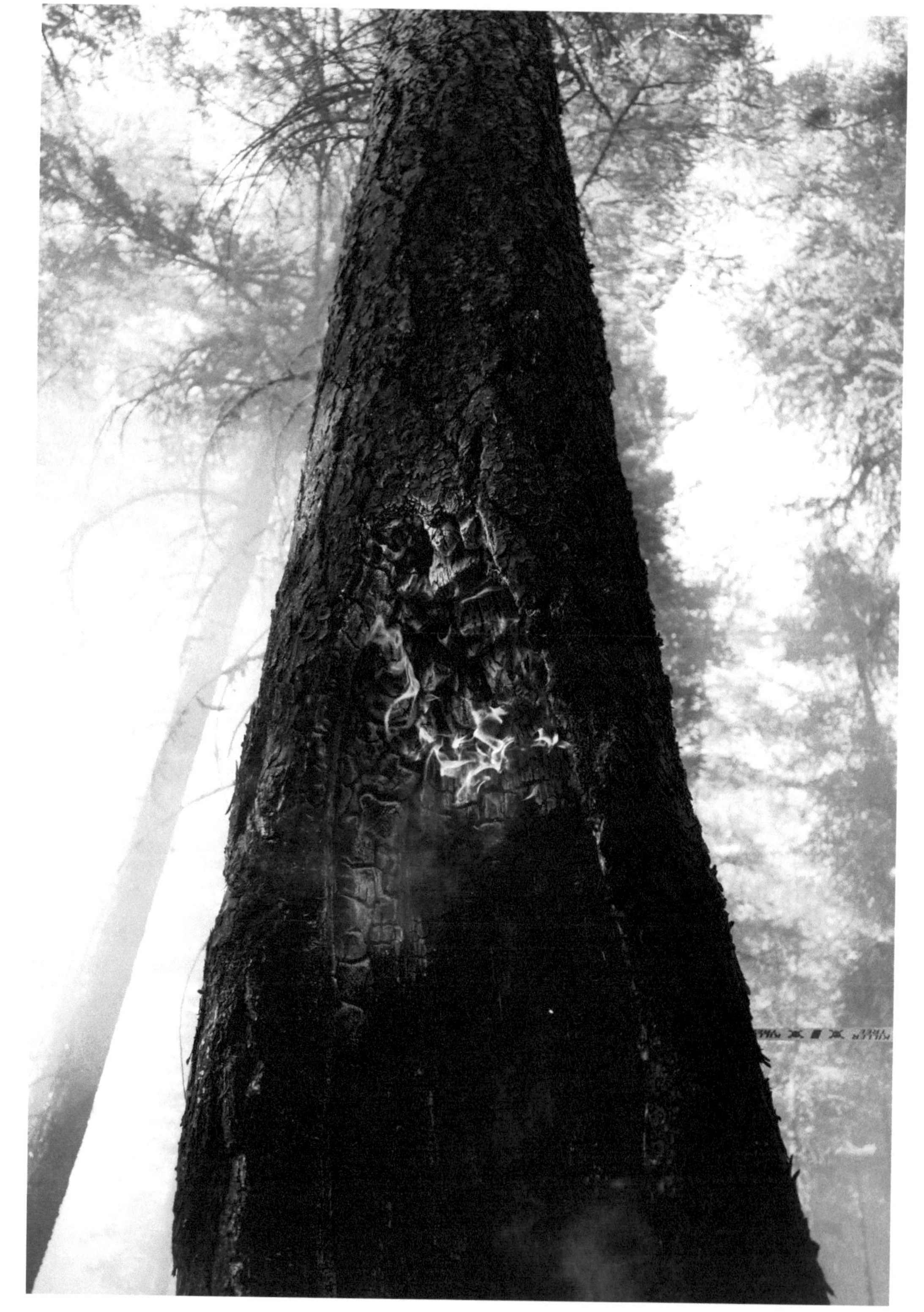

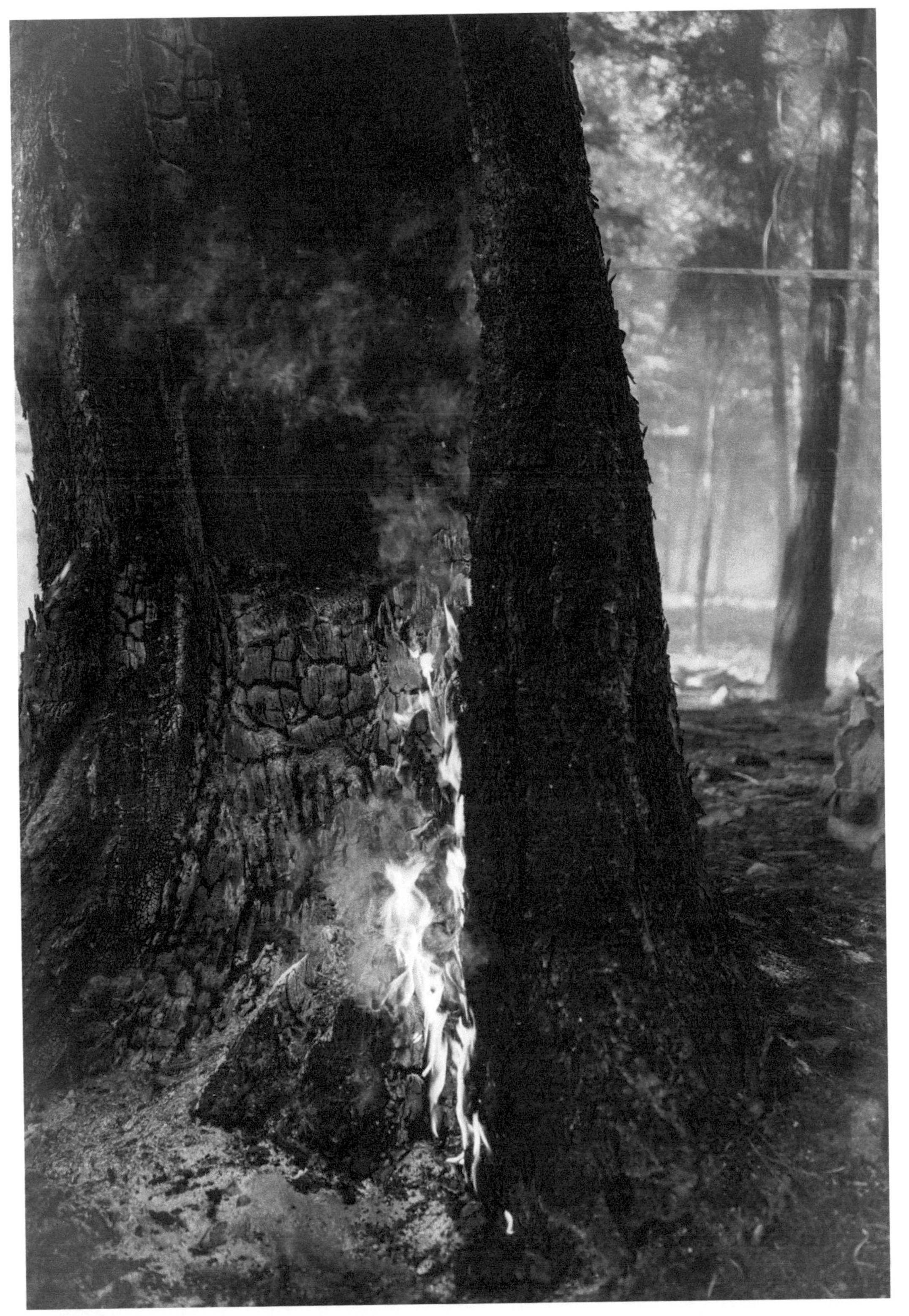

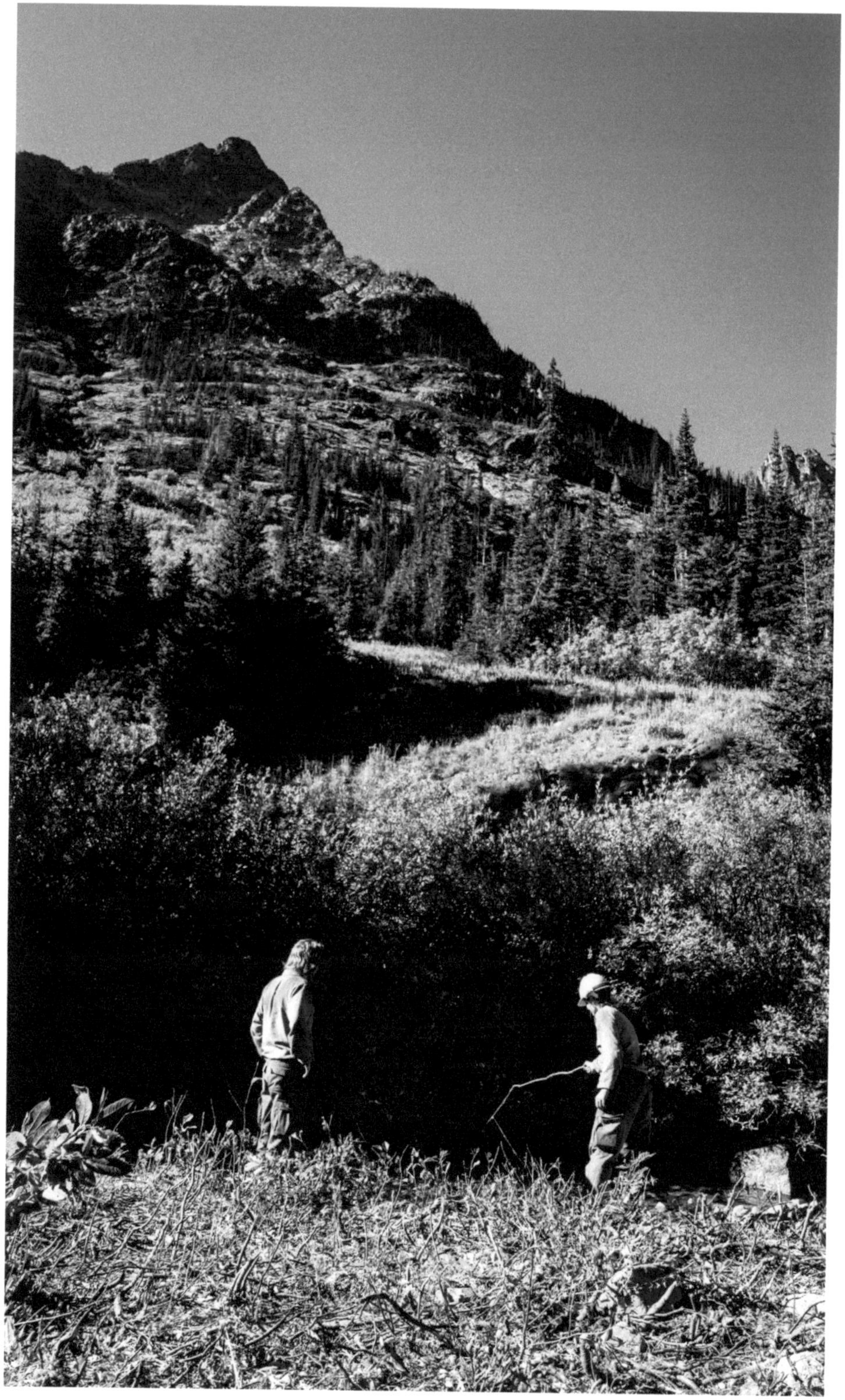

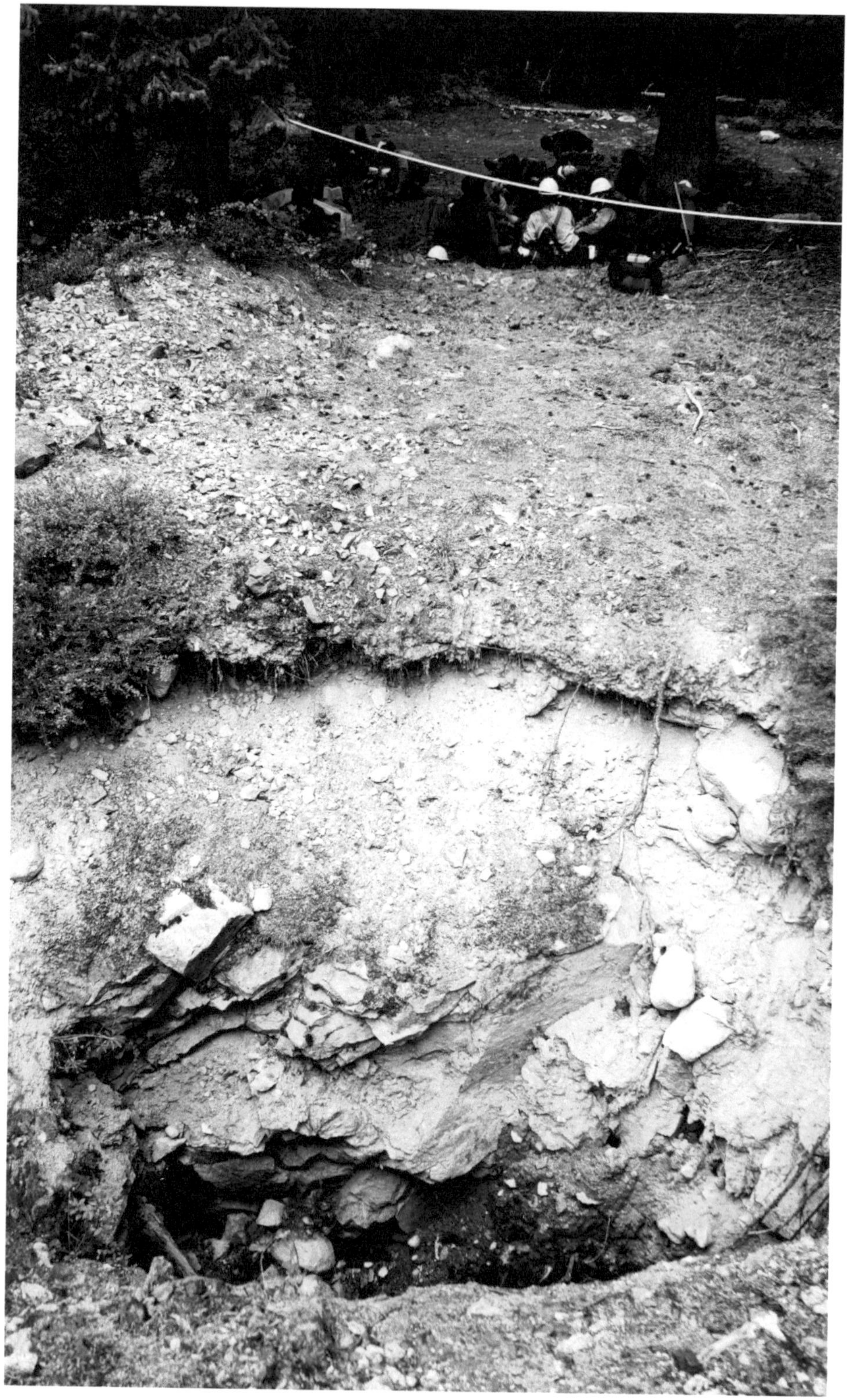

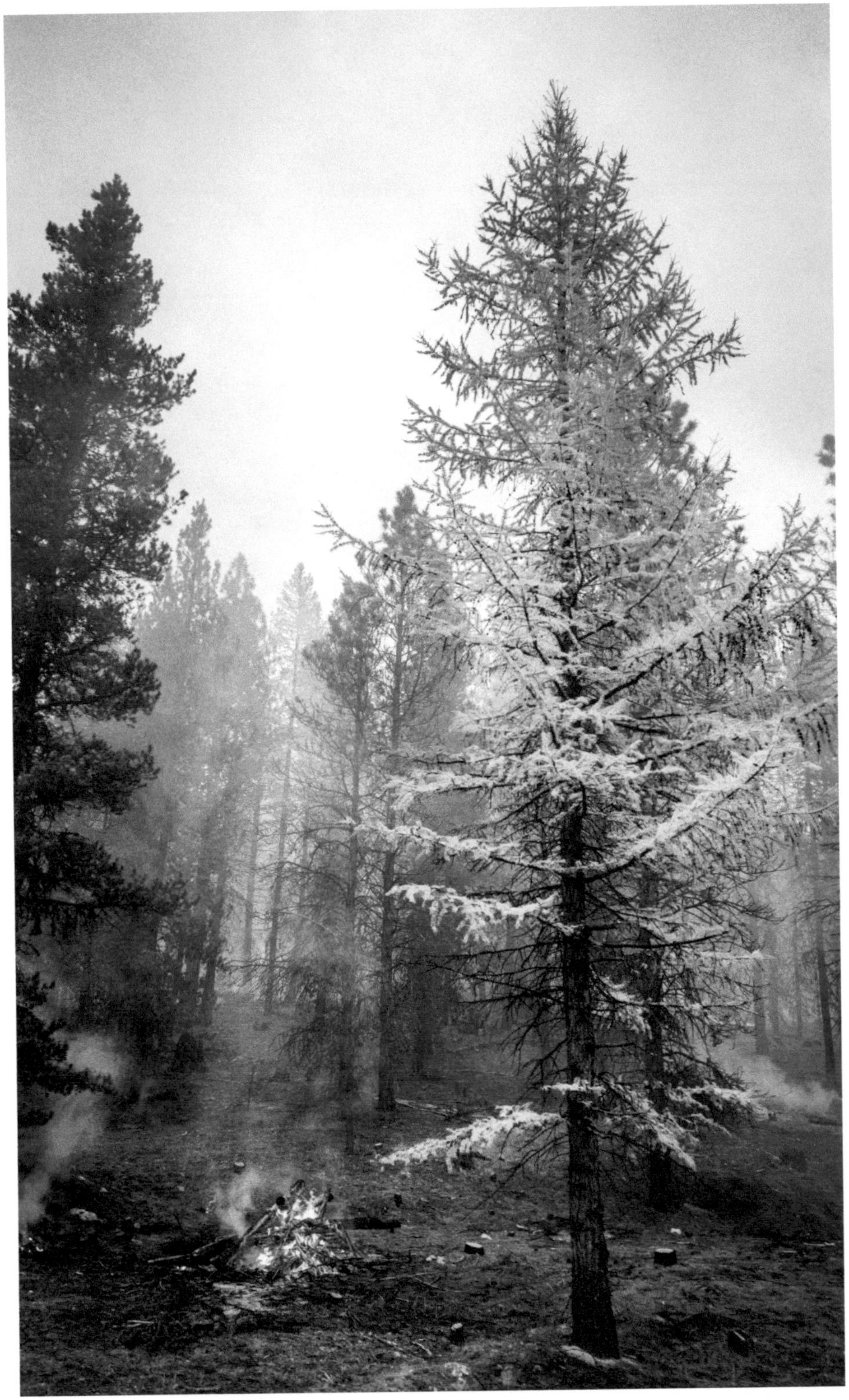

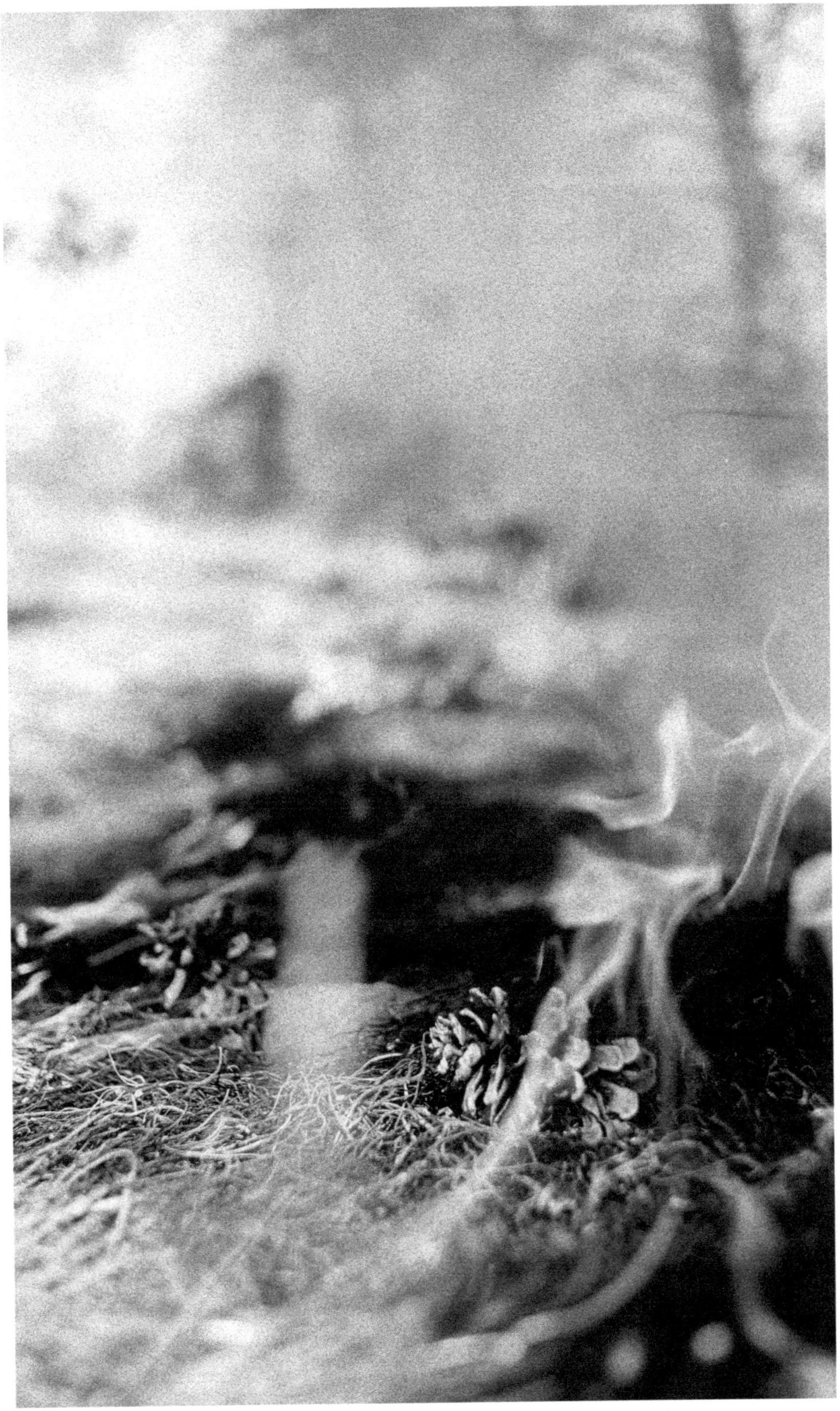

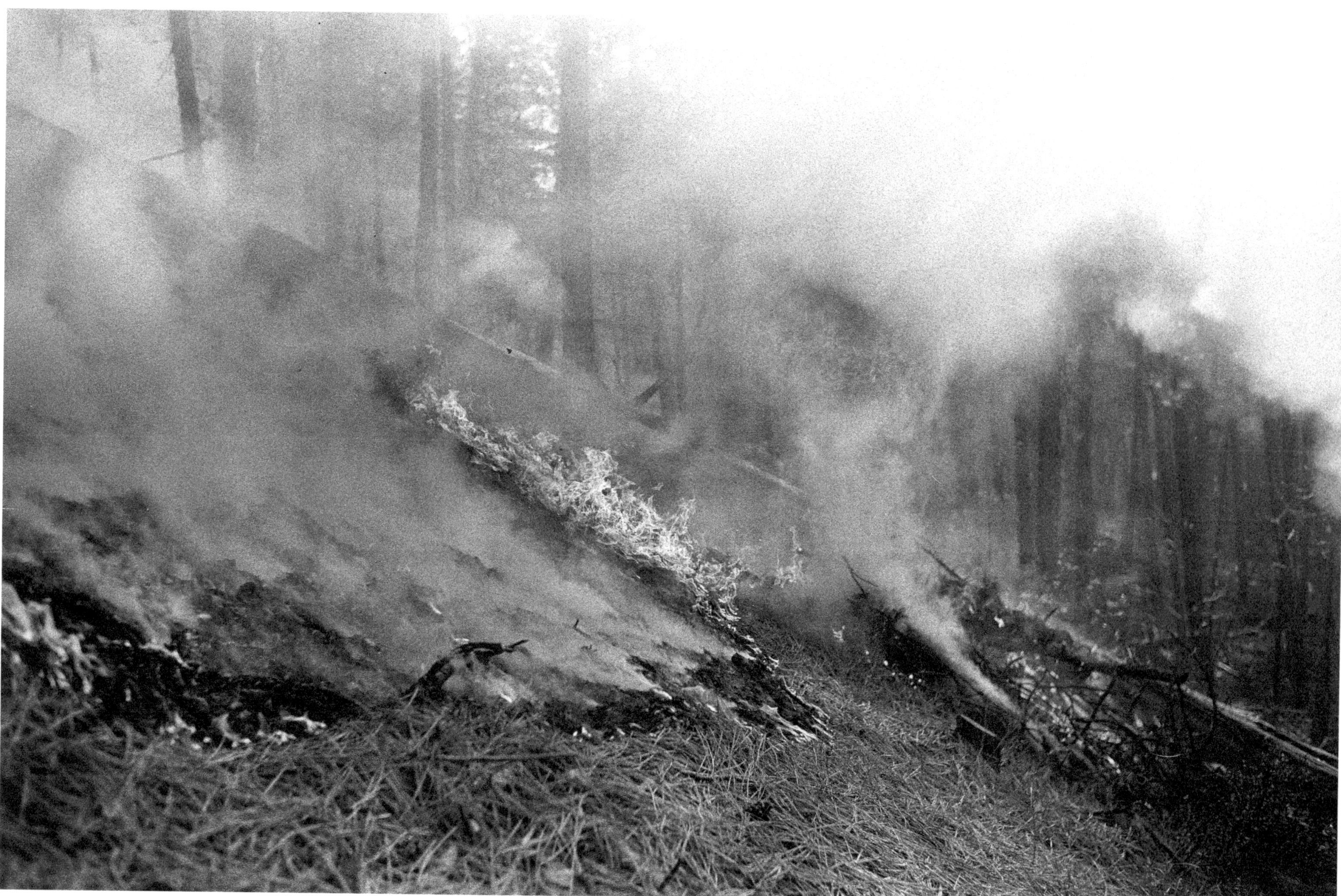

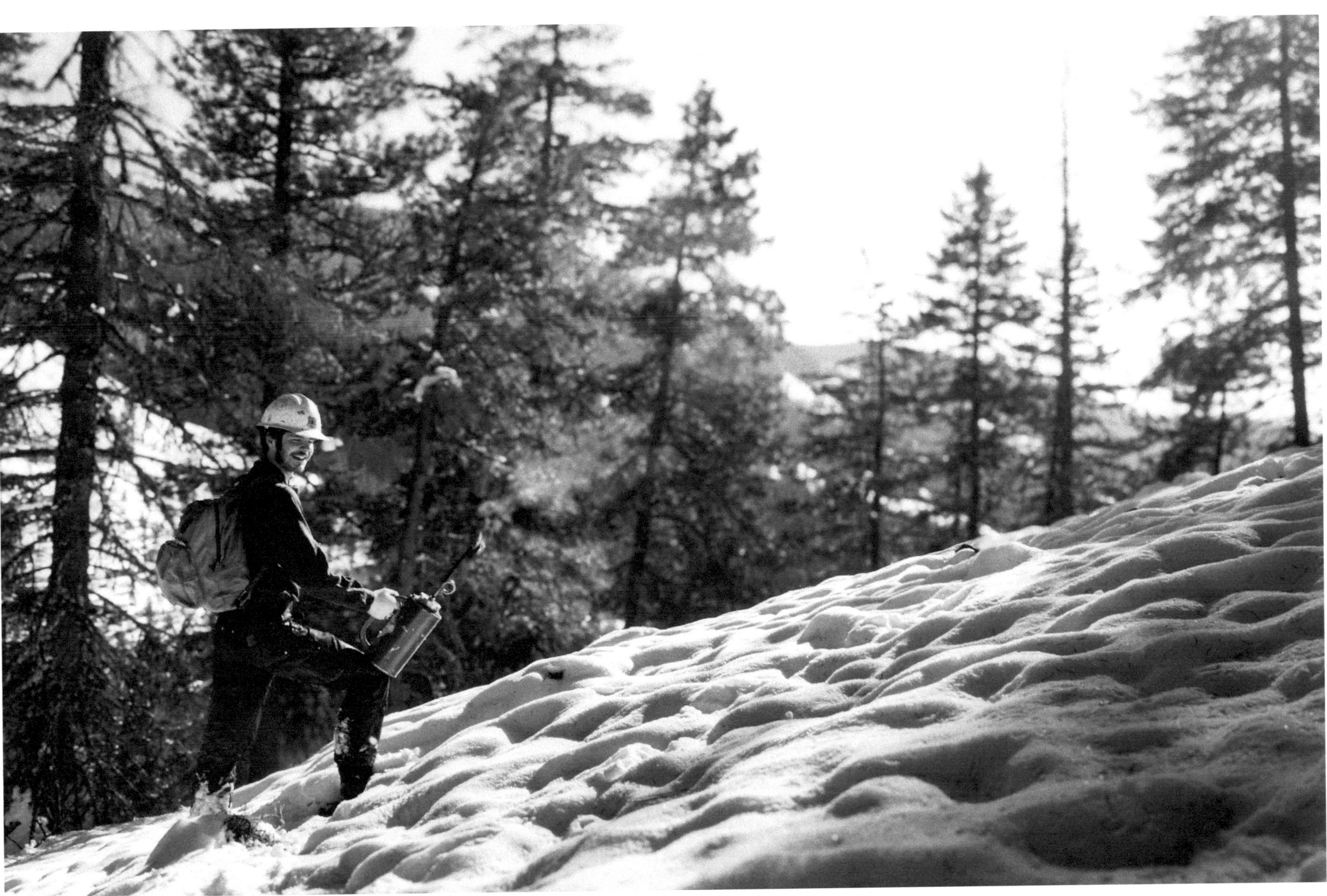

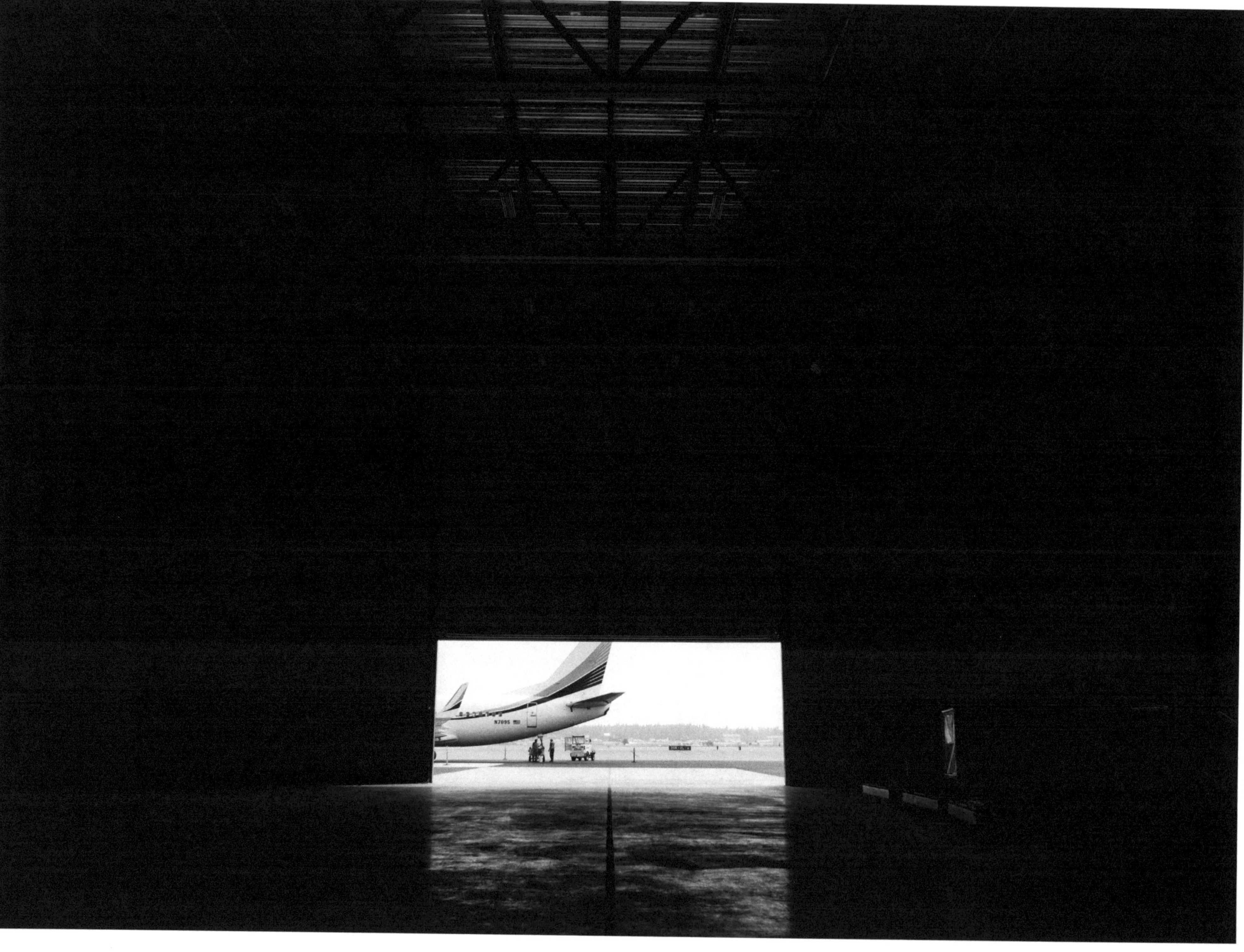

III.

The final photo of the airplane hangar has developed more meaning for me over time. Initially, it was simply, "Wow, this is stunning." The soft light bleeds through the bay door from a smoked-out Alaskan sky. The overall feeling is one of excitement for the new landscape as we arrived at this dismal scene in Fairbanks. Before the crew was shuttled off in a school bus, I looked back through the hangar and took this shot.

Two years later, I now reflect on the photo itself. That was the first eight months I had committed myself to being out of service, or at least having an excuse to stick my head in the sand. Eight months committed to wearing one pair of boots. Eight months committed to missing birthdays and anniversaries of those you love. Eight months postponing health appointments. Eight months as an enigma, unable to describe my experiences to friends and family back home, and maybe a little unrecognizable to them too. Eight months on your résumé that, if not documented properly, will not help you with any pay raise. Eight months where you hope for the best fire assignments, and when you make it, you complain about them anyway.

I look back on my experience with awe at what many beside me, before me, and after me have given up to be right there, chopping away at the dirt next to me—a small flame inside that combusts with the will to do something bigger, greater than ourselves.

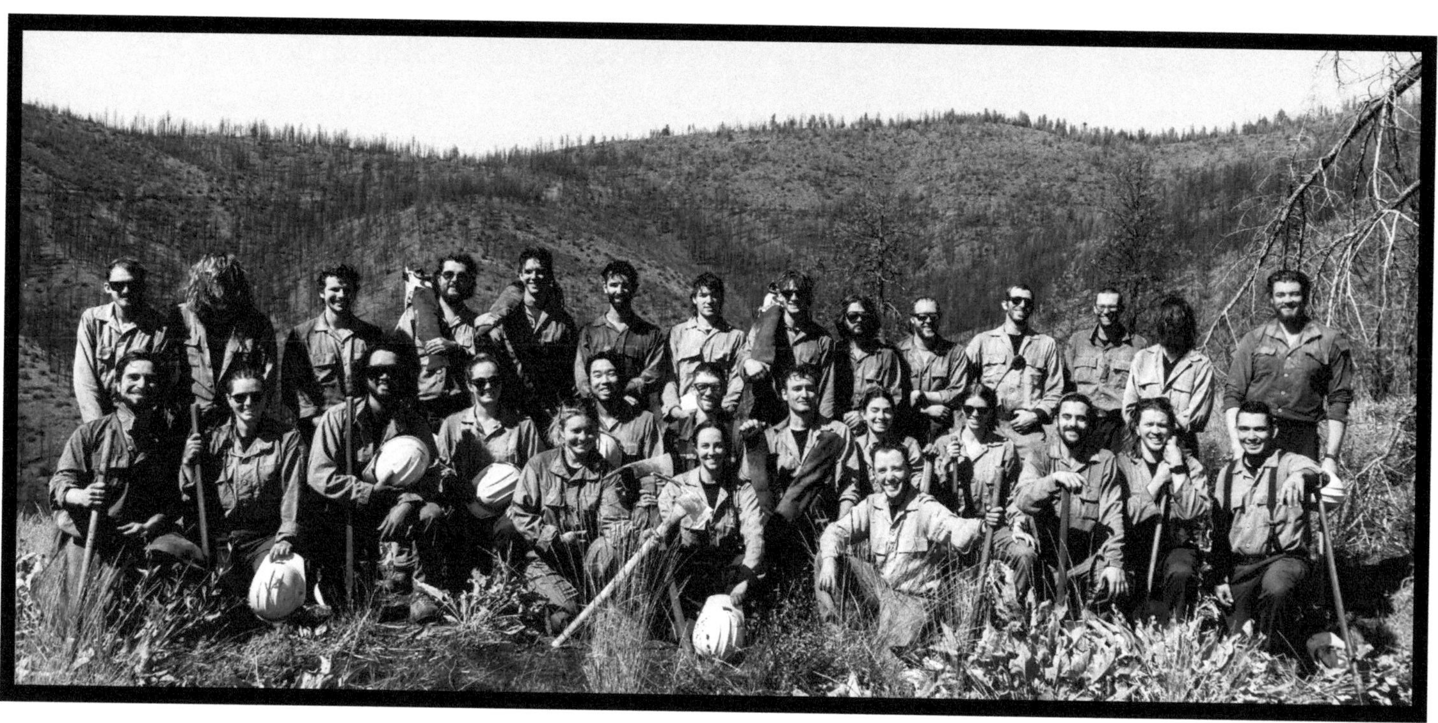